Savor

the {

southwest

Savor
the southwest

Barbara Pool Fenzl with Jane Horn

Foreword by **Jacques Pépin**

Photography by Frankie Frankeny

Based on the public television series

BAY
BOOKS

San Francisco

This book is published to accompany the public
television series *Savor the Southwest*. This series is a
production of KAET-TV, Phoenix, Arizona

Bay Books is an imprint of Bay Books & Tapes, Inc.,
555 De Haro St., No. 220, San Francisco, CA

Designed by Rey Int'l/IntersectionStudio
Food Photography by Frankie Frankeny
Illustrations by Richard Sala
Landscape Photography: The Image Bank © 1999;
    cover and pg. 56, Daniela Schmid; pg. 2, Marc
    Romanelli; pg. 4, S. Brooks Bedwell; pg. 16, Paul
    McCormick; pg. 40, Marc Solomon; pg. 78,
    Lawrence McFarland; pg. 122, William Stickney;
    pg. 146, Joseph Devenney; pg. 162, Charles C.
    Place; pg. 190, Carlos Navajas
Author photo by Jorgen Larson
Copy Editor: Ken Della Penta
Proofreader: Sabrina Rood-Sinker
Indexer: Ken Della Penta

Library of Congress Cataloging-in-Publication Data

Fenzl, Barbara.
    Savor the Soutwest / Barbara Pool Fenzl with
Jane Horn; photography by Frankie Frankeny.
        p.   cm.
    Includes index.
    ISBN 0-912333-70-7 (pbk. : alk. paper)
    1. Cookery, American—Southwestern style.
        I. Horn, Jane, 1945-
. II. Title.
TX715.2.S69F48 1999
641.5979—dc21   98-53656
                                 CIP

ISBN 0-912333-70-7
Printed in China
10 9 8 7 6 5 4 3 2
Distributed by Publishers Group West

Contents

Foreword by Jacques Pépin

I remember many years ago when I was working in France, and later when I first came to this country as a young chef, my palate had little tolerance for spicy foods. At that point in my career, I wouldn't have believed that later on in my life I would differentiate between chipotle, jalapeño, poblano, and Scotch bonnet peppers. Hot, spicy ingredients seem to grow on you, and in the last twenty years, with exposure to diverse cuisines, from Szechuan to Thai to Vietnamese—but, especially, to Mexican and Southwestern cooking—my palate has come to love hot food in all different forms. It has grown on me so much that I long for it, and have to have my "fix" several times a year.

When I hear the call of the poblano, I head out to Phoenix to visit my friend, Barbara Fenzl, an expert on Southwestern food, and get my full measure of piquant and eye-watering food. My wife, Gloria, and I wait each year for the addictive chiles she sends us; in the ultimate spirit of friendship, Barbara finds, roasts, and peels them for us, then sends them all ready to be placed in a jar with garlic and oil or mixed into different dishes. This petite, vivacious, attractive woman, author of *Southwest the Beautiful Cookbook*, is not only an authority in the kitchen but has a knack for bringing chefs together and for explaining the rules of cooking in simple, coherent, well-thought-out words.

In a new series on public television and in this companion cookbook, *Savor the Southwest*, Barbara has assembled the top-notch chefs of the region, from Vincent Guerithault to Robert Del Grande to John Sedlar to Chuck Wiley to Robert McGrath, to name but a few. She is the *vox populi*, asking, probing, and explaining the chefs' recipes to us, the audience, clearly defining what Southwestern cooking is. A mix of Mexican, Native American, Spanish, and European, Southwestern cooking, with its unique local ingredients, is an original, exciting cuisine that has been an important player in the revolution underway in American cuisine and American restaurants in the last few years.

The scope of Southwestern cuisine is, indeed, quite vast. It is not limited to chili con carne, tortillas, and jalapeño peppers. This book will seduce you with complex, sophisticated dishes, such as Roasted Yellow Pepper Soup with chile cream, Achiote-Basted Rack of Venison, Contemporary Chicken Mole, and Cornmeal-Crusted Sea Bass with Corn and Tomatillo Salsa. The classics, however, have not been forgotten: Splendid recipes for Guacamole, Black Beans with Chipotle, Shrimp Quesadillas, Blue Corn Bread, and Flour Tortillas are waiting to delight your guests.

So, wake up your taste buds, give your friends a treat, get behind the stove, and start cooking Southwest. There is fun, freedom, and excitement in these recipes. Happy Cooking!

Acknowledgments

This book is dedicated to my husband, Terry, and our three children, whose love and support sustain me in all I do.

This project would never have happened without the vision of Jillian Robinson, manager of program development and production at KAET-TV. I am forever grateful for her insight, friendship, and faith in me. And my heartfelt thanks also go to Beth Vershure, Chuck Allen, Patti Jay, Joe Campbell, Suzanne Stock, and the rest of the terrific staff at KAET-TV for their support and expertise.

A generous grant from the Ethel and Kemper Marley Foundation made the series possible. I hope the series—and this book—will be a lasting reminder of the late Ethel Marley's love for Arizona.

The creativity, humor, and excellence of the production crew of A La Carte Communications is evident in the television shows, and my special thanks go to Geoffrey Drummond for his unflappable, upbeat attitude and wise guidance; to Nat Katzman for his counsel and business acumen; to Bruce Franchini for his artistic eye and insightful direction; to Ashley Hathaway for her command of the details; to Chris Styler, our hero in the prep kitchen, for his infinite patience, and to his helpers Pat, Andrew, and Melissa; to Gilles Morin, our sound expert, for his Gallic esprit and geniality; to Eliat Goldman for his technical wizardry; to Dean Gaskill, Steven Hussar, Ben Avechuco, and Tommy Hamilton for their terrific camera work; and to the lovely Clara Taillole-Nardo for her hair and makeup artistry and her constant good cheer. What a team!

I'm especially grateful to the creative, skilled chefs who participated in the series. They shared their inspired recipes, gave up precious time to travel to Prescott, Arizona, for the taping, and showed remarkable patience and humor during the entire television and book-writing process.

A huge thank you goes to Hillary Guild and her husband, Don, for allowing us to take over their beautiful Southwestern home in Prescott for the two weeks of taping the shows. Not only were they generous hosts—they were also tireless workers, pitching in whenever we needed them.

I'm always indebted to my friend and assistant, Linda Hopkins, for letting me explore ideas with her and for her constant encouragement and support. Thank you to Linda, Patti Hart, and Kim Howard for testing all the recipes in this book and giving me valuable feedback.

Jane Horn was my valued collaborator on this book. Thank you, Jane, for the clarity of your vision, the skillfulness of your pen, and your many large and small contributions that have given shape to this book—but most of all for your friendship and delightful sense of humor.

Introduction

Here in the Southwest, we not only claim the oldest regional cuisine in the United States, but we also have changed the way America eats. Salsa, not ketchup, is now America's favorite condiment. Look at me—I'm a peanut-butter-and-jelly girl from the Midwest. "The best thing since sliced bread," we liked to say. But then I moved to the Southwest thirty years ago and made its table my own. Today, my sandwich is as often on a tortilla as bread from a loaf. And if the nationwide wrap craze is any indication, so is yours.

In Illinois where I grew up, but just as easily in Maine or Georgia or Idaho, I can buy tortillas at most groceries (along with chiles, jicama, cactus pads, and prickly pear fruit). The whole Southwestern kitchen has even crossed the Atlantic. In London I came across two restaurants with a Texas theme. A fish and chips burrito? PB&J in a wrap? Not likely, but certainly possible!

Encompassing austere deserts, rugged mountains, fertile valleys, and endless plains, the Southwest is not easily pigeonholed. Neither is its food. Early Mexican settlers introduced chocolate, chiles, and tomatoes. The Anasazi Indians millennia ago grew what their descendants, the Pueblo Indians, eventually cultivated as corn, squash, and beans—the holy trinity of Southwestern ingredients. With the arrival of the Spanish in the 1500s, wheat and cattle added flour, meat, milk, and cheese to the regional pantry. The fruit orchards of European missionaries and later Anglo settlers soon flourished. Now modern-day transplants that flock to the Sunbelt bring their special foods and customs.

So, toss out the myth that Southwestern cuisine is a recent, trendy creation. Until even twenty years ago, food was still prepared in ages-old fashion with local ingredients. Recipes were handed down generation to generation. Posole, a toothsome stew of hominy, pork, and chiles revived winter-weary appetites at New Year's festivities in Santa Fe. Carne seca, the precursor to beef jerky, was cured in the hot Tucson sun as a way to preserve meat. Chili con carne, the famous "bowl of red," fueled hardworking cowboys on the trail. All share a humble and very insular beginning: Few people outside the region, or from one county to the next, for that matter, were aware of these dishes that are now so commonplace.

But our secret got out. A revolution of sorts was underway in American restaurants in the late 1970s and early 1980s. "Fresh, local, creative" was the rallying cry. The Southwest responded, led by Santa Fe–born John Rivera Sedlar. At St. Estèphe, near Los Angeles in Manhattan Beach, he blended French training with his native New Mexican heritage and named it "modern Southwestern cuisine." At about the same time, Vincent Guerithault was adding prickly pear sorbet to his classic repertoire in an oasis in the middle of the desert north of Phoenix. In Tucson, Janos Wilder was cooking at his restaurant with chiles and produce harvested from his own garden. Elsewhere, Stephan Pyles in Dallas, Robert Del Grande in Houston, and Mark Miller in Santa Fe were making headlines with their own unique spins.

To outsiders who viewed Southwestern cooking as little more than fast food with a burn, the new regional style was a revelation. Given impeccably fresh local ingredients, this cadre of creative, energetic Southwestern chefs produced dazzling results: lobster tacos, cactus French fries, thick stews made with heirloom beans, and chocolate jalapeño sundaes. The food world ate it up.

Today, more than a decade later, it's not just foodies who rush to eat at this new Southwestern table. It appeals to anyone who seeks fresh, colorful, full-flavored cooking sparked with some chile power. Nor is it just a regional passion. Chefs everywhere are combining their local ingredients with such Southwestern staples as chiles, cilantro, tomatillos, and wild game. Meanwhile, Southwestern chefs cross regional borders to experiment with foods from the Tropics and from Asia, cuisines that also thrive on spice and heat.

Sit down to our table yourself. Let this cookbook introduce you. Included are all the recipes demonstrated by the fourteen talented chefs who appear with me on *Savor the Southwest*, plus more from their personal recipe files and many from my own. They require no special skills for success; everything is clearly explained. Many of the recipes are followed by a "chef's tip"—accompanied by the portrait of the chef—advice on techniques or ingredients that will help ensure success. Do-ahead tips precede most recipes. Check the extensive glossary, too, for a complete description of ingredients and important techniques.

You'll also find the recipes easy to shop for at most supermarkets. The Southwestern pantry, from chiles to chayote, is now widely available. And what you can't pick up in person, specialty mail-order catalogs can rush to your door in just days. Organized by course, the recipes mix and match into menus that are simple in spirit, yet robust in flavor—a good description of the Southwest itself.

What excites me most about modern Southwestern cooking is the way it welcomes change, but also honors and preserves its past. That's why I close every show with the clang of the traditional chuck wagon triangle: Come savor the Southwest. Come and get it!

—Barbara Pool Fenzl

Meet the Chefs

Robert Del Grande

The most important part of Southwestern cuisine is its subtlety—not outrageous spiciness or stereotypes of enchiladas and tamales—but subtle flavors and perfumes and textures that seem to make the cuisine ineffable. This is what is most important and is often missed—the very fine shadings that give the region its soul.

If cooking is as much science as art, Robert Del Grande is doubly skilled. With two science degrees, including a Ph.D. in biochemistry, he not only knows how to create the innovative cuisine that wins raves for Houston's Cafe Annie and Rio Ranch, but why it all works so well. Del Grande is a Californian by birth but adopted the Lone Star State and its cuisine as his own when he met and married his wife, Mimi. In 1981 he traded laboratory science for kitchen science to cook at Cafe Annie, owned by Mimi's sister and brother-in-law. Del Grande had some restaurant experience (he cooked to help pay graduate school bills), but even so, his success as a chef was meteoric: In a year he was running the kitchen. Still in charge at Cafe Annie, at Rio Ranch since 1992, and also co-owner of eight Texas branches of Cafe Express, he is consistently ranked as one of America's top chefs. The James Beard Foundation named him Best Chef: Southwest in 1992.

Vincent Guerithault

I think the future holds strong for Southwestern cooking as it has proved that it is more than a passing food fad. I believe it will remain especially strong in the Southwest, where the ingredients that are its foundation are found in abundance. Southwestern cuisine as we now know it will become more sophisticated and less rustic as we become more acquainted with combining these regional flavors with other foods.

French-born Vincent Guerithault has put Phoenix on the map, foodwise, with his eponymous restaurant. But when he first moved to Pinnacle Peak from Le Français in Wheeling, Illinois in 1979, to run the kitchen at Oaxaca, he experienced culinary culture shock. For this classically trained chef, not only was the restaurant in the middle of nowhere, but it offered French food and tortillas on the same menu. Guerithault flourished cooking side by side with Mexican chefs. By the time he opened Vincent's six years later, these new regional nuances were seamlessly blended with his classic French repertoire. Author of *Vincent's Cookbook*, he is the 1993 winner of The James Beard Foundation's Best Chef: Southwest Award. Guerithault has been featured in the *New York Times*, *Los Angeles Times*, *Gourmet*, *Bon Appétit*, *Travel and Leisure*, and on the cover of *Money*.

Jay McCarthy

It is just great to observe how Southwestern cuisine is evolving. As chefs get more access to the unusual chiles and exotic produce like cactus pears and pitaya, it is fun to watch the creative process weave these different ingredients on the plate. All you have to do is have a Cactus Rita to see how colorful the future of Southwestern cuisine can be. *Bien provecho.*

Cactus Rita is not Annie Oakley's sidekick. It's a magenta margarita that gets its dark red hue from cactus pear purée, and the invention of "Cactus King" Jay McCarthy (the recipe is on page 38). Currently McCarthy is the acclaimed chef at Harmon's in Telluride, Colorado, but cactus is his obsession: He is the president of the Professional Association of Cactus Development and a world expert on the prickly plant. Born in New York, he grew up in Jamaica on his family's spice plantation, then took a degree in aeronautical engineering at Texas A & M University. But cooking, not rockets, captured his interest. He left the aerospace field and trained in restaurants in New York and Palm Beach before moving back to the Southwest; first to Texas and spots at Polos at the Fairmont, Zuni Grill, and San Antonio's prestigious Cascabel; and now, Colorado.

Robert McGrath

The Southwest region of the United States is typified by a boldness of spirit and the ability to pioneer new directions. It only makes sense that the cuisine of the Southwest personifies these characteristics— food that reflects the integrity of the balance of nature and that is also fun to prepare and fun to eat. Southwestern cuisine is not a ceremony; it's a celebration!

You don't get peanuts with your cocktail at Roaring Fork, Robert McGrath's restaurant in Scottsdale, Arizona. It's trail mix and jerky, the same victuals he snacks on while camping, fishing, rafting, or hiking with his family every summer in Colorado. In fact, Roaring Fork is named for his favorite river near Aspen, and the Great Outdoors is its theme. McGrath's cuisine, which he calls "American Western," reflects his lifelong love for the food and spirit of the frontier West. Praised for its wit—and McGrath's obvious skill in making it all work—the menu is part chuck wagon, part campfire, part fine dining. Prior to Roaring Fork, McGrath was chef de cuisine at Windows on the Green at Scottsdale's Phoenician resort and Four Seasons hotels in Houston and Austin, and chef and owner of Sierra Grill in Houston. In 1988, *Food and Wine* named him one of the Ten Best New Chefs in America, and he was four times a nominee—1994, 1995, 1997, and 1998—of The James Beard Foundation for Best Chef: Southwest.

Mary Sue Milliken and Susan Feniger

We fell in love with Mexican flavors while working in French kitchens with Latino prep cooks. They'd whip up a terrific salsa in seconds flat, and we wanted to know how. Our curiosity and appetite for these complex tastes led us to look at Mexican influences in this country—from Rancho California to the Southwest, where so many cultures converge. This food is as good as it gets—anywhere in the world.

If you ask Mary Sue Milliken and Susan Feniger about the French Revolution, they might just tell you it took place not in Paris, 1789, but in Chicago, 1978. They made culinary history in the Windy City that year as the first women to work in Le Perroquet's formerly all-male French kitchen. Training in France followed, with their own restaurant back in the States the goal. In 1981, they jointly opened the popular City Cafe in Los Angeles. With the Border Grill in Santa Monica, the pair married two of their culinary passions—classic French and the bold flavors of Mexico and Central America. Their latest collaboration, Ciudad, which opened in downtown Los Angeles in late 1998, serves urban Latin foods from all over the world. A second Border Grill is set to debut in Las Vegas in June 1999. In 1988, the California Restaurant Writers Association named them jointly Chef of the Year. Milliken and Feniger host television's *Too Hot Tamales* and the radio show *Good Food*.

Donna Nordin

It's hard for me to believe that when we opened Cafe Terra Cotta in 1986, there were no real "Southwestern" restaurants in Arizona. Yes, we had cowboy steak houses. And yes, we had a variety of mainstream cuisines with a touch of jalapeño and a sprig of cilantro. So I said, "Let's go right to the heart and make Cafe Terra Cotta contemporary Southwestern." You know what? The first year we had to tell people our food was California cuisine with chiles. Today, after twelve years and well over one million Cafe Terra Cotta customers, they don't have to ask, and we don't have to tell. Southwestern cuisine speaks for itself with much pizzazz!

As an expert on cooking in general, and chocolate in particular, Donna Nordin's destiny may well have been the Southwest long before she arrived in Tucson from San Francisco in 1984. Chocolate is one of the region's signature ingredients, and for a time Nordin toured extensively on behalf of a top chocolate manufacturer. She also headed her own Bay Area cooking school. While a guest teacher at a culinary school in Tucson, she not only fell in love with Arizona, but also the school's director, Don Luria. They married and together opened two Cafe Terra Cotta restaurants (Tucson and Scottsdale) and Tucson's Tohono Chul Tea Room. The also have a nationally distributed line of culinary products. Nordin trained in France at Le Cordon Bleu and Ecole Le Nôtre. *Contemporary Southwest*, her first cookbook, showcases her modern, imaginative regional cuisine. In 1993, she was a James Beard Foundation nominee for Best Chef: Southwest.

Loretta Barrett Oden

The flavors of the Southwest are quite unique. Many of the ingredients date back hundreds, even thousands, of years to the brilliant agriculturists who were the indigenous peoples of the Americas. This extraordinarily rich and diverse bounty has traveled far and has impacted the cuisines of the world: Tomatoes! Potatoes! Corn! Chiles! Chocolate! Vanilla! . . .to name just a few. As for the food now referred to as "Southwestern," it, too, is traveling far afield. I am witnessing the exciting, no-holds-barred creativity of today's adventurous chefs, taking the once "exotic" tastes of the Southwest to glorious new heights.

Loretta Barrett Oden was raised near the Potawatomi Reservation in Shawnee, Oklahoma, in a family long active in tribal politics (her brother has chaired the Citizen Potawatomi Nation since 1985). In Santa Fe, New Mexico, Oden opened Corn Dance Cafe, praised by *Food Arts* as "a year-round Native American feast," to share her passion for the native foods of the Americas. Over 90 percent of the ingredients used in the cafe kitchen are indigenous to the New World, much bought from Native American suppliers. Before she opened her restaurant, Oden undertook a three-year, cross-tribal odyssey to seek out the traditional recipes that now inspire her cuisine. Outside of the cafe, Oden lectures and holds workshops on indigenous crops and traditional cooking methods and consults throughout the Indian community.

Stephan Pyles

When I first began practicing Southwestern cuisine some fifteen years ago, my efforts were concentrated on creating a new style of cooking based on the ingredients and traditions inherent in the American Southwest, including New Mexico and Arizona. As a fifth-generation Texan, my focus has shifted to reinterpreting existing recipes of my state and creating new dishes that would help shape the cuisine of Texas into the next century. My current style of cooking, New Texas Cuisine, is based on ethnic and cultural influences specific to the Lone Star State.

With a degree in music, Stephan Pyles's career path seemed set. But a food-filled, post-college trip to France convinced him that as much as he loved music, he loved cooking more. Restaurants were familiar territory: His family owned the Truck Stop Cafe in West Texas, and by age eight, he was already a fixture there. He perfected his culinary skills in a number of Dallas restaurants, then opened the acclaimed Routh Street Cafe in 1983, followed by its more casual sibling, Baby Routh. At Star Canyon, his current venue, the menu celebrates his Texas roots—a mix of cowboy, Southern, and Southwestern influences, plus (by his own count) a few dozen more. Pyles is also chef and partner at AquaKnox, where his creative seafood reels in even dedicated Dallas carnivores. Hailed as a founding father of Southwestern cuisine, Pyles was named Best Chef: Southwest in 1991 by The James Beard Foundation. He's also a member of Who's Who of Food and Beverage in America. He is the author of *The New Texas Cuisine* and coauthor of *Tamales.* He hosts the nationally syndicated public television cooking show *New Tastes from Texas* and authored the companion book of the same name.

Lenard Rubin

Southwestern cuisine is here to stay. It's just as much a "fad" as is the Southwest itself. There are many different styles and interpretations, some of which possibly originated from the Southwest of Mars or thereabouts. In any case, what really matters are the ingredients: chiles, beans, corn, and of course, cilantro, to name a few of the staples. Call the final product what you will—people have cooked with these ingredients for centuries and will for many more. The people, places, styles, and interpretations are ever changing, with no end in sight. Southwestern cuisine will continue as long as we respect and nurture the ingredients. I am proud to be part of that culture.

During his stint as opening chef at Windows on the Green at Scottsdale's Phoenician resort, Lenard Rubin's enthusiasm for cilantro and other Southwestern ingredients got him dubbed "The Cilantro King." But his passion for regional flavors developed earlier. As sous chef at The Boulders Resort in 1986, and then at the Piñon Grill, his menus favored local ingredients and flavors. Rubin's other title could well be roving regional culinary ambassador: From Alaska to Malaysia to Moscow, Rubin has fired up diners the world over with his lively Southwestern cooking. Rubin is currently chef de cuisine at the Marquesa, Scottsdale Princess Resort.

Roxsand Scocos

Southwestern cuisine for me is yet to be defined. Is it Mexican, is it Cowboy Grub, is it Wagon Train, or Stage Coach food? The possibilities are pretty exciting. For me, however, its foundation is based on what is coming off the vine and out of the earth, and when.

Roxsand Scocos has been recognized by *Gourmet*, *Esquire*, and *USA Today* as one of America's most unique and talented chefs at one of the most innovative restaurants in Arizona— RoxSand. Her dynamic dishes reflect the diverse elements of her culinary training, and she has recently begun introducing Native American ingredients to her menu selections. First a painter and sculptor, Scocos switched her artistic medium to cooking almost twenty years ago when she opened RoxSand Patisserie and Cabaret in Hawaii. A tour as pastry chef at The Boulders Resort in Carefree, Arizona, followed, with her own RoxSand—winner of numerous awards for dining excellence—opening in Phoenix in 1986. Four years running, 1995 to 1998, Scocos was nominated by The James Beard Foundation as Best Chef: Southwest. Her restaurant is a three-time winner, 1996 to 1998, of *Gourmet's* America's Top Tables award.

John Rivera Sedlar

When I first began serving tortillas, tamales, and chiles in a fine dining environment, people gasped. Now, fancy and casual restaurants alike showcase these ingredients and dishes in places of high honor on their menus.

John Rivera Sedlar began his professional career in his native New Mexico, but it was in California that his unique cuisine attracted national attention. In 1980, he opened St. Estèphe in Manhattan Beach, the first restaurant to feature contemporary dishes made with Southwestern ingredients. In Los Angeles, he named his next venture Abiquiu, for the New Mexico city that was home to the late artist Georgia O'Keeffe (Sedlar's aunt was her cook). There, his menus continued to express his creativity, incorporating spices and ingredients not just from the Southwest, but from all over the world. Sedlar is generally recognized as the father of modern Southwestern cuisine. His ground-breaking cookbook, *Modern Southwest Cuisine*, is a classic that has been recently updated and rereleased. Sedlar is a member of Who's Who of Food and Beverage in America and the youngest chef ever to receive the *Food Arts Silver Spoon Award*.

Janos Wilder

I came to Tucson after working in Bordeaux and wanted to cook French food. I had to answer the question, "How do you cook French food with cilantro, chiles, prickly pears, and beans?" For fifteen years, my menus have been an attempt to answer that question.

To this French-trained chef, the garden is the heart and soul of cooking. In fact, it was for gardeners first, then staff, that Janos and Rebecca Wilder advertised when they planned their first Tucson restaurant in 1982, set in an historic 1865 home. Wilder is chef and owner of Janos, a trend-setting restaurant now in its own building on the grounds of the Westin La Paloma, with a panoramic view of the Tucson valley. His cooking style is French, but expressed with local ingredients. He harvests from his own garden for his restaurant (a concept he pioneered in the area) or turns to local farmers to supply what he can't grow. Six years in a row—1992 to 1997—he was nominated by The James Beard Foundation as Best Chef: Southwest. His restaurant is a consistent winner of the AAA Four Diamond and Mobil Four Star awards. Wilder is the author of *Janos: Recipes and Tales from a Southwest Restaurant*.

Chuck Wiley

My interpretation of Southwestern cuisine began with a deep reverence for the centuries-old fare of Mexico, borrowing culinary notions from South America and the Caribbean. Happily this style of cooking is more approachable than ever for the home cook, with America's expanding markets and love for the fragrance of mesquite, garlic, cilantro, roasting chiles, corn tortillas, and oregano.

Chuck Wiley still cooks in the wide-open spaces with a Dutch oven and a Griswold skillet. But it's a Harley, not a horse, that gets this modern-day cowboy to the back country. Wiley is executive chef of The Boulders Resort in Carefree, Arizona; The Lodge at Ventana Canyon in Tucson; The Peaks in Telluride, Colorado; and Carmel Valley Ranch in California. Expertise at grilling and smoking meats, fish, and vegetables are among his many talents, and his innate sense of flavor combinations earns Wiley and his cuisine national acclaim. In 1994 *Food & Wine* named him one of the Ten Best New Chefs in America. He was also honored by The James Beard Foundation as one of America's Best Hotel Chefs.

Chapter 1

Appetizers

Most people think of the Southwest as a dry, arid desert—red rock country full of reptiles and coyotes. But, in fact, it's a beautiful, bountiful garden that yields not only tomatoes, squash, and corn, but exotics like chayote, chiles, and prickly pears.

Around most of Texas, and much of the Southwest, the spiny prickly pear cactus is part of the landscape and lore. For all those who malign it as a pesky intruder better chopped down, others celebrate its feisty—and flavorful—qualities. In fact, Texas named it State Plant in 1995, a honor long overdue according to folks like "Cactus King" chef Jay McCarthy, creator of such innovations as the Cactus Rita (a prickly pear margarita, see page 38) and Cactus Fries (see page 130). As president of the Professional Association for Cactus Development, McCarthy enthuses over its many virtues: It is high in vitamin C and fiber and low in fat, with promising medical potential. Mostly though, McCarthy cooks with cactus because he's just wild about its taste. But he's not the first to see the edible gifts that hide beneath its prickly demeanor. The Aztecs enjoyed it as both food and beverage, and Columbus carried the fruit—called tunas—back with him to Europe. Certain desert-dwelling Southwestern Indian tribes depended on the moisture-filled thick pads—nopales—and the sweet juice from the tunas for survival during times of severe drought.

Befitting its newfound respect, cactus and cactus foods, from pickles to purées to jams to spreads, are in demand, and cactus is a cultivated crop. You can buy fresh pads and the brilliant red fruit in most Southwestern markets and in specialty groceries in other parts of the country.

Inspired by another of nature's gifts to the Southwest—corn—is one of the region's most beloved holiday foods—tamales. It takes no great leap of imagination to picture an ear of corn in its papery husk and then see it as a homey, corn-based dish wrapped in a dried husk and steamed until moist and flavorful. Tamales have been served since ancient times on feast days. In the Southwest, they're a treasured Christmas tradition, and making them is a family affair. Marathon sessions involve the best family cooks, assisted by a hardworking corps of daughters, aunts, cousins, and friends who gather in a central kitchen to beat the corn masa dough until it's so light that a pinch floats in a glass of water.

Fillings of beef, chicken, and pork are traditional, but marry tradition with a creative bent and you have John Rivera Sedlar's elegant French-inspired Salmon Mousse Tamales (see page 30) garnished with edible blossoms or his extraordinary Chocolate Tamales with Candied Chiles (see page 175).

Chefs like McCarthy, Sedlar, and Roxsand Scocos, chef/owner of RoxSand, in Phoenix, Arizona, rely on local growers as much as possible for the farm-fresh ingredients from cactus to corn that are a signature of their modern Southwestern cuisine. Scocos is a passionate promoter of locally grown produce and has developed strong working relationships with area farmers. Says Scocos: "When you're buying locally, and in season, you're buying the best." Her commitment to the freshest ingredients finds tangible expression in her Mesquite Crêpes with Onion Filling and Leek Broth (see page 34).

This chapter of enticing appetizers draws from the bountiful Southwestern garden, plus a harvest of other fresh, exciting ingredients. They'll turn any occasion into a Southwestern fiesta. So rev up the margarita machine (as Jay McCarthy calls his blender), ring up a few friends, and start cooking.

Eggplant Tostaditos

Makes 16 to 20 pieces

Tortillas, not eggplant, are the usual foundation for tostaditos—typically layers of refried beans, shredded meat, and garnishes. But there's nothing usual about this elegant, bite-sized appetizer, which also works as a terrific side dish for meat or poultry. Pepitas, the pumpkin seeds of the Southwest, and earthy, smoky poblano chiles infuse the pesto with regional gusto.

Pumpkin Seed Pesto

2 poblano chiles, roasted, peeled, and seeded
½ cup fresh basil leaves
½ cup olive oil
½ cup freshly grated Parmesan cheese
½ cup pepitas (pumpkin seeds), lightly toasted
½ cup spinach leaves, thoroughly washed
½ teaspoon salt
2 cloves garlic

1 eggplant, preferably a Chinese or other long variety, 2 to 3 inches in diameter
1 to 2 tablespoons olive oil
Salt and freshly ground black pepper to taste
1 cup crumbled cotija cheese (substitute Monterey jack)
4 red bell peppers, roasted, peeled, seeded, and cut into julienned strips
1 tablespoon finely chopped cilantro

Do Ahead { The pesto can be made up to 2 days ahead of time, tightly covered, and refrigerated.

For the pesto: Combine all ingredients in a food processor and pulse until the mixture is semicoarse.

Preheat an oven to 350°. Slice the eggplant into rounds about ⅛-inch thick. Spread the olive oil over the surface of a baking sheet. Place the rounds on the oiled pan and turn over so each side of the eggplant slices are lightly oiled. Season with salt and pepper to taste. Bake until the slices soften and begin to brown slightly, 10 to 15 minutes. Let cool.

Spread half of the eggplant rounds with pesto. Layer the remaining ingredients over the pesto in the following order: cheese, red pepper strips, and cilantro. Top the rounds with the remaining eggplant slices, forming sandwiches.

To serve as an appetizer: If the rounds are small enough, leave whole; otherwise, cut each into halves or quarters, depending on how large the eggplant rounds are, so that each tostadito is bite-sized.

To serve as a vegetable side dish: Place 1 large or 2 small rounds on each plate to accompany meat or poultry dishes.

Beef Nachos

In the Southwest, nachos range from a snack topped with just cheese and chiles to a more substantial appetizer like this one. Pickled jalapeños are found in the condiment section of most grocery stores. They're quite hot, but they add just the right amount of pizzazz to the meat mixture. The pungency of commercial chile powders can vary from brand to brand, so find one whose heat suits your palate.

½ pound lean ground chuck
1 tablespoon freshly squeezed lime juice
2 tablespoons finely chopped red onion
1 tablespoon finely chopped pickled jalapeño chiles
¼ teaspoon salt
¼ teaspoon chile powder
¼ cup finely chopped cilantro
1 cup grated queso fresco, cotija, or Monterey jack cheese
40 tortilla chips
½ cup sour cream, for garnish
40 fresh cilantro leaves, for garnish

Do Ahead The nacho mixture can be made up to 4 hours ahead of time, covered, and refrigerated. Bring to room temperature before spreading on tortilla chips.

Preheat a broiler.

In a bowl, stir together the beef, lime juice, onion, jalapeños, salt, chile powder, cilantro, and cheese. Gently spread each tortilla chip with a thin layer of the mixture (about 1 tablespoon per chip). Place on a baking sheet and broil 6 inches from the heat until the meat is completely cooked and the cheese is melted, 3 to 4 minutes.

Top each nacho with a dollop of sour cream and a cilantro leaf. Place the finished nachos on a serving platter and serve immediately.

Arizona Crostini

Makes about 40

Are these Italian nachos or Southwestern crostini? A little of both, probably, as the Mediterranean trio of basil, olives, and garlic all grow in Arizona gardens. Latino markets are a good source for the crumbly, tangy Mexican cotija cheese.

¾ cup grated cotija cheese
   (substitute asiago)
2 tomatoes, seeded and diced
1 tablespoon finely chopped
   garlic
20 kalamata olives, pitted and
   finely chopped
¼ cup coarsely chopped fresh
   basil
1 baguette, cut into ¼-inch-
   thick slices

Do Ahead { Without adding the basil, the cheese mixture can be made up to a day ahead of time, covered, and refrigerated. The basil should be added just before spreading the mixture on the bread slices.

Preheat a broiler.

With a fork, mix together the cheese, tomatoes, garlic, olives, and basil.

Place the bread slices on a baking sheet and broil 6 inches from the heat until lightly browned. Remove from the broiler and turn the bread slices over so the soft side is up. Press about a tablespoon of cheese mixture onto the untoasted sides of the bread. Return the pan to the hot broiler and cook until the cheese is melted and the edges of the bread are toasted, 2 to 3 minutes. Serve immediately.

Stuffed Jalapeño "Mice"

John Rivera Sedlar

Makes 16

These darling appetizers look meek, but roar in your mouth. The cheese counteracts most of the heat, but there's still a nice bite to the finish.

½ cup crumbled feta cheese
1 tablespoon extra virgin olive oil
1 teaspoon finely chopped garlic
1 teaspoon coarsely chopped
   fresh oregano
¼ teaspoon freshly ground
   black pepper
7 kalamata olives, pitted and
   coarsely chopped

Do Ahead { These can be stuffed a day ahead, covered, and refrigerated.

In a small bowl, with a fork mix together the feta, olive oil, garlic, oregano, pepper, and 6 of the chopped olives until well blended. Cover and refrigerate while preparing the chiles.

With the tip of a small, sharp knife, slice each chile open lengthwise from the base of its stem to the tip, leaving the stem attached. Open it up flat and remove the seeds and ribs. Lightly salt the inside of each chile.

16 jalapeño chiles, roasted and
  peeled
Salt to taste

With a teaspoon, neatly mound the filling in the center of each chile,
distributing it evenly. Close the sides of each chile around the filling.

Place the chiles, seam side down, on a small serving platter, all point-
ing in the same direction like scurrying mice. With the pieces of
reserved chopped olive, give each mouse two little black eyes, pressing them gently into each chile near its narrow tip, opposite the stem
(tail) end. Serve immediately.

Filled Tortilla Wedges

Makes 24

**In New Mexico, tortillas are stacked, not rolled, with plump fillings supporting the layers.
These are substantial hors d'oeuvres, or a toothsome garnish for a first-course salad. You
couldn't find a better way to recycle leftover chicken or turkey.**

1 cup finely chopped cooked
  chicken
1 cup cooked black beans (if
  canned, rinse thoroughly)
1 cup cooked corn kernels
1 cup diced red onion
2 poblano chiles, roasted,
  peeled, seeded, and diced
1 cup cotija cheese or queso
  fresco, crumbled
1½ cups Monterey jack cheese,
  grated
Salt and freshly ground black
  pepper to taste
1 tablespoon Achiote Paste (see
  page 205)
4 tablespoons unsalted butter
6 flour tortillas, 7 to 8 inches in
  diameter

**Do
Ahead** { The tortilla stacks can be prepared up to a
day ahead, covered, and refrigerated.

In a large bowl, toss together the chicken, black beans, corn, onion,
chiles, and cheeses. Season to taste with salt and pepper.

In a blender or food processor, purée the achiote paste and the butter. In the microwave or over low heat, melt the achiote butter.

Place 1 tortilla on a work surface. Brush 2 teaspoons achiote butter
onto the tortilla. Spread one-fourth of the chicken mixture evenly
over the tortilla. Top with a second tortilla and brush it with 2 more
teaspoons achiote butter; spread it with another fourth of the mixture. Top with a third tortilla. Repeat with the remaining tortillas and
filling so there are 2 tortilla stacks. Cover and refrigerate until ready
to use or transfer to a baking sheet.

Preheat the oven to 400°. Brush the tortilla stacks with the remaining
achiote butter. Bake until the cheese is melted and the tortilla stacks
are warmed, 10 to 15 minutes. Remove from the oven and cut each
stack into 12 wedges. Serve immediately.

Squash Blossom Quesadillas

Serves 4 as an appetizer

The Pueblo peoples of the Southwest not only enjoy the vibrant yellow-orange squash blossom as a food but revere it as a religious symbol in their ceremonies. Serve the quesadillas cut in large wedges for a meal or bite-sized wedges as appetizers. Vary the presentation by mixing plain flour tortillas with flavored ones such as tomato, spinach, or pepper, or use a variety of cheeses.

4 fresh squash blossoms
1 tablespoon unsalted butter
1 shallot, finely chopped
Salt and freshly ground black pepper to taste
1 cup shredded mild cheese such as Monterey jack or queso blanco
2 flour tortillas, 8 inches in diameter

Wash and drain the squash blossoms. Remove and discard the stems and cut the blossoms into strips.

In a small skillet, melt the butter over medium heat. Add the shallot and cook until softened, about 4 minutes. Add the squash blossom strips and sauté another minute. Season with salt and pepper to taste.

Arrange half the cheese over one-half of a tortilla. Top with half the squash blossom mixture and fold the tortilla in half. Repeat with the second tortilla and remaining cheese and filling.

Place a large skillet over medium-high heat. When the pan is hot, place the filled tortillas in the dry pan. Cook until lightly browned on 1 side, about 1 minute; turn over and cook until the second side is lightly browned and the cheese is melted, another 1 to 2 minutes. Cut each quesadilla into 4 wedges and serve immediately.

The Mozzarella Company of Dallas makes a delicious, mild queso blanco that beautifully complements the delicate quality of the squash blossoms. You can order their cheeses by mail (see Mail-Order Sources, page 217).

Shrimp Quesadillas

Serves 6 to 8 as an appetizer

Munched on by children all over the Southwest for lunch or as snacks, quesadillas are the Mexican equivalent of grilled cheese sandwiches. The base is always a flour tortilla, and the filling is always cheese, but then anything goes. This version adds shrimp and chile sauce to the equation.

½ pound shrimp (32 to 36 per pound), cooked, peeled and deveined

½ cup Red Sauce (see page 197) or Chipotle Sauce (see page 194)

1 cup water

1 small white onion, halved and thinly sliced

2 poblano chiles, roasted, peeled, seeded, and cut into strips

2 cups grated Monterey jack cheese

6 flour tortillas, 8 to 10 inches in diameter

With a sharp knife, cut the shrimp in half lengthwise along their backs. In a bowl, toss the shrimp with sauce. Set aside.

In a small skillet, bring the water to a boil over high heat. Add the onion slices and remove the skillet from the heat. Let the onions stand in the water until wilted and softened, about 10 minutes. Drain and set aside.

Divide the shrimp, onions, chile strips, and cheese evenly over half of each tortilla. Fold the tortillas in half. Heat a nonstick skillet over medium heat until the skillet is very hot. Brown the filled tortillas on both sides in the dry skillet. Cut each quesadilla into 4 to 6 wedges and serve immediately.

 You don't need oil to cook quesadillas, but the skillet must be hot enough to melt the cheese filling. A standard 10-inch skillet can cook two quesadillas at a time if they're arranged in the pan folded sides facing.

Cactus Shrimp with Butter Sauce

Jay McCarthy

Serves 4 appetizer servings

The jewel-toned magenta prickly pear purée and the ochre achiote paste give these shrimp beautiful color. Prickly pear fruit is usually sold denuded of its spines, but have thick gloves on hand to handle them just in case a few are left.

Prickly Pear Batter

4 prickly pear fruit (tunas), peeled
1 cup packaged tempura mix
1 tablespoon Achiote Paste (see page 205)

Butter Sauce

¼ cup white wine
1 shallot, finely chopped
¼ cup heavy cream
½ cup unsalted butter, cut into 8 pieces

Peanut oil for frying
¼ cup cornstarch
½ pound shrimp (26–30 per pound), peeled and deveined

For the batter: Place the prickly pear fruit in a food processor or blender and pulse until the pulp is broken up. Strain through a sieve with holes large enough to hold back the seeds but let most of the pulp through. Measure out 1 cup of purée and place in a bowl. (Freeze the remainder for another use.) Place the tempura mix and achiote paste in the blender or food processor and purée until smooth. Add to the bowl with the prickly pear purée. Mix well and refrigerate until chilled, about 30 minutes.

For the sauce: In a saucepan over medium heat, cook the wine and shallot until the wine is almost gone (about 1 teaspoon left). Add the heavy cream. Reduce the heat and simmer, whisking constantly, until the cream is somewhat thickened, 3 to 5 minutes. Remove from the heat and allow to stand for 5 minutes. Slowly whisk in the butter, one piece at a time, until the sauce is smooth. Keep warm, but do not reheat or the sauce will separate (a thermos works well).

Fill a heavy skillet with peanut oil to a depth of 2 inches. Heat the oil over medium-high heat to 375°. Place the cornstarch on a shallow plate and remove the prickly pear batter from the refrigerator. Dip each shrimp into the cornstarch, then the batter, and fry in the hot oil, 3 or 4 shrimp at a time, until golden brown, about 5 minutes. Drain on paper towels.

Assembly: Divide butter sauce among 4 plates. Arrange 3 or 4 fried shrimp attractively on each plate. If desired, serve with Cactus Fries (see page 130).

Shrimp in Red Chile Cream Sauce

Landlocked Arizonans looking for some sand and sea head for the laid-back beach town of Puerto Penasco (Rocky Point) in Baja, California, a four-hour drive from Phoenix. As a last stop before they head home, vacationers fill a cooler with delicious Rocky Point shrimp, caught in local waters and sold frozen at local markets.

Sauce

- 1 cup water
- 1 dried New Mexico red chile, stemmed, seeded, and cut into strips
- 1 Fresno red or Hungarian cherry pepper, stemmed, seeded, and diced
- ⅓ cup diced red bell pepper
- ⅔ cup diced white onion
- 1 teaspoon finely chopped garlic
- 1 teaspoon cumin seed, toasted and ground, or ¾ teaspoon ground cumin
- Salt and freshly ground black pepper to taste
- ⅓ cup heavy cream

- 2 tablespoons vegetable oil
- 2 pounds shrimp (26 to 30 per pound), peeled and deveined
- 1 tablespoon freshly squeezed lime juice
- 6 sprigs fresh parsley, for garnish

Do Ahead { The sauce can be made up to 2 days ahead, covered and refrigerated.

For the sauce: In a small saucepan over high heat, bring the water to a boil; remove from the heat and add the dried chile strips. Soak for at least 30 minutes. Add the diced fresh chile, bell pepper, onion, garlic, and cumin to the saucepan. Return the pan to medium heat; bring the mixture to a boil, reduce the heat, and simmer for 15 minutes. Cool slightly and purée the mixture in a blender until smooth. Pour the mixture back into the saucepan. Add salt, pepper, and cream and put the pan back over medium heat; simmer for another 15 minutes. Remove from the heat and keep warm.

In a large skillet, heat the oil over medium-high heat. Season the shrimp with salt and pepper to taste and add them to the hot pan. Sauté the shrimp until they just turn pink, about 2 minutes. Sprinkle the lime juice over the shrimp.

Divide the sauce among 6 shallow bowls or rimmed plates; top each bowl with 9 or 10 shrimp. Garnish with a sprig of parsley and serve with warm tortillas.

To peel shrimp: Loosen the shell along the shrimp's underside, then pull it off with a tug of the tail. **To remove the black vein:** Cut along the outer curve of the peeled shrimp with a small knife, then pick out the vein.

Silver Dollar Crab Cakes on Corn Pancakes

Makes 32

Generous amounts of chile in the cornmeal pancake batter, in the seafood mixture, and in the chipotle sauce root this version of an East Coast favorite firmly in the Southwest. The pancakes are also delicious simply topped with a piece of smoked salmon and a dollop of sour cream, crème fraîche, or Mexican Cream (see page 203).

Corn Pancakes

½ cup yellow cornmeal
¼ cup all-purpose flour
½ teaspoon salt
1 teaspoon baking powder
1 teaspoon sugar
⅛ teaspoon hot pepper sauce
1 egg white
½ cup beer
2 tablespoons finely chopped green onion, white and light green parts
2 tablespoons finely chopped celery
1 jalapeño chile, stemmed, seeded, and finely chopped

Crab Cakes

1 cup Chipotle Mayonnaise (see page 204)
1 tablespoon Dijon mustard
1 tablespoon freshly squeezed lemon juice
1 large egg, lightly beaten
1 pound lump crabmeat, picked over and patted dry
1 cup fresh bread crumbs
¼ cup finely chopped green onions, white and light green parts
1 teaspoon finely grated lemon zest
½ teaspoon salt
1 tablespoon unsalted butter
1 tablespoon corn oil
About 32 cilantro leaves

Do Ahead { The pancakes can be made a day ahead of time and stored in an airtight container.

For the corn pancakes: In a bowl, mix together the cornmeal, flour, salt, baking powder, and sugar. In a small bowl, mix together the hot pepper sauce, egg white, and beer. Add the wet ingredients to the cornmeal mixture; fold in the onion, celery, and jalapeño. Heat a large nonstick skillet over medium heat and spray lightly with nonstick cooking spray. Drop the batter by tablespoonsful into the pan, forming circles 1½ inches to 2 inches in diameter. Cook until golden brown, turning once. Remove and cool on a wire rack.

For the crab cakes: In a bowl, whisk together ¼ cup of the chipotle mayonnaise, the mustard, lemon juice, and egg. Stir in the crab, bread crumbs, onions, lemon zest, and salt. Form into 2-inch cakes (about 1 tablespoon mixture each). In a nonstick skillet, melt half the butter and oil together over medium heat. Cook the crab cakes in batches until brown and cooked through, about 2 minutes per side, adding more butter and oil when necessary.

Assembly: Place 1 crab cake on top of each corn pancake. Top with a dollop of the remaining chipotle mayonnaise and a cilantro leaf.

Salmon Mousse Tamales with Edible Flowers

John Rivera Sedlar   Serves 8

These elegant tamales with their contemporary spin epitomize John Rivera Sedlar's modern Southwest cuisine and pay homage to his New Mexico heritage. The flowers were inspired by the work of artist Georgia O'Keeffe, who lived in Sedlar's hometown of Abiquiu, and infuse the tamales with some of their fragrance. Edible flowers are available in many grocery stores.

Tamale Dough

½ pound fresh masa, or ¾ cup masa harina mixed with ½ cup water
1 tablespoon vegetable shortening
½ teaspoon salt
¼ teaspoon baking powder
⅛ teaspoon white pepper
2 to 3 tablespoons chicken stock, at room temperature

Salmon Mousse

1 pound fresh salmon, trimmed and cut into 1-inch pieces
1⅓ cups heavy cream
1 teaspoon salt
1 teaspoon white pepper
1 whole egg
1 egg white

Assorted fresh herbs and pesticide-free edible flowers (chives, chervil, basil, sage, thyme, nasturtiums, pansies, violets, rose petals)
16 dried corn husks, soaked in warm water for at least 2 hours

For the tamale dough: Bring the masa and vegetable shortening to room temperature. Place masa, shortening, salt, baking powder, and pepper into the bowl of an electric mixer fitted with the paddle attachment. Mix the ingredients for 5 minutes on low to medium speed, occasionally cleaning the sides of the bowl with a rubber spatula. Continue mixing while slowly drizzling the chicken stock into the bowl for another 3 to 4 minutes. The masa should not be too wet.

For the salmon mousse: Place the salmon, cream, salt, and pepper into the bowl of a food processor. Purée for 1 minute, stopping a few times to scrape the bowl. Add the egg and egg white and process 1 more minute to make a firm, dense mousse mixture. The mixture should be free of any ligaments or fat; if any are visible, press the mixture through a fine sieve with a rubber spatula.

Assembly: For each tamale, place a 6 x 12-inch sheet of plastic wrap on the work surface. Spread a very thin layer of tamale dough in a 1½ x 3-inch rectangle in the center of the plastic wrap. Mound about ⅓ cup mousse on top of the masa. Place a bouquet of assorted herbs and flower petals to simulate a floral arrangement on top of the mousse. Remove 8 husks from the water, clean, and pat dry. Cut a 1½ x 3-inch rectangle from each of the 8 corn husks and place on top of the flower/mousse layer. Bring the plastic wrap up and around the husk to seal the tamale in a neat package.

Bring a large pot of water to a boil over high heat. Place a steaming rack on top of the boiling water and place the tamales, husk side down, on the rack. Cover and steam until firm to the touch, 8 to 10 minutes. While the tamales are steaming, remove the remaining 8 husks from the water, clean, pat dry, and tear a ¼-inch strip from the edge of each one. Tie one end of each husk with the strip to make a boatlike shape.

Place a corn husk boat on each of 8 plates. Unwrap the plastic wrap from each tamale. Lift the corn husk off the salmon mousse. Carefully place a tamale into each corn husk boat, floral side up.

Smoked Trout Spread

Makes about 2 cups

The Southwest is crisscrossed with rivers that yield to the persistent fisherman the most mouthwatering trout. Your own smoked trout makes this seasoned spread a particular delicacy, but reeling in the catch from a fish market or specialty store is fine, too.

Trout

2 trout (6 to 8 ounces each), cleaned and filleted, skin still on

1 teaspoon freshly squeezed lemon juice

Salt and freshly ground black pepper to taste

2 tablespoons wood chips, soaked in warm water for at least 30 minutes

Spread

1 tablespoon unsalted butter

2 teaspoons finely chopped garlic

2 tablespoons finely chopped shallot

½ cup dry white wine

2 tablespoons freshly squeezed lemon juice

1 (8-ounce) package cream cheese

Salt and freshly ground black pepper to taste

Toasted baguette slices, crackers, or raw vegetables, for accompaniment

Do Ahead { The trout can be smoked up to 3 days ahead, wrapped well, and refrigerated. The spread can be made 2 days ahead, covered, and refrigerated.

For the smoked trout: Sprinkle the trout with the lemon juice, salt, and pepper. Sprinkle the wood chips on the bottom of the smoker and place the drip tray on top of the chips. Place the food rack on top of the drip tray and arrange the trout on the rack. Place the smoker on medium heat with the lid off and the handles open for use. When the wood begins to smolder, close the lid and start the cooking time. Cook for 20 to 25 minutes, until the flesh is cooked through. Let cool.

For the spread: Remove the skin from the smoked trout and break the trout into pieces; set aside. In a small skillet, heat the butter over medium heat. Add the garlic and shallots and cook until soft and translucent, 3 to 4 minutes. Add the wine, raise the heat to medium-high, and cook until the liquid is reduced to about ¼ cup, about 5 minutes. Transfer the mixture to a blender or food processor. Add the lemon juice, cream cheese, and smoked trout. Purée and add salt and pepper to taste. Serve with toasted baguette slices, crackers, or raw vegetables.

Pepper Jelly Pinwheels

Makes about 28

In the Southwest, pepper jelly is a "hot" condiment for its mix of sweet and heat. It's quite easy to make and a terrific gift. For a very simple hors d'oeuvre, spoon about ½ cup of jelly over an 8-ounce package of cream cheese and serve with wheat crackers. This is a variation of that popular appetizer.

3 whole-wheat tortillas, 9 inches in diameter

1 (3-ounce) package cream cheese, softened

3 tablespoons Pepper Jelly (see below)

½ cup chopped toasted pecans

Do Ahead { The tortilla rolls can be made up to 2 days ahead. Cut into slices just before serving.

Lay the tortillas out on a work surface. Spread each tortilla with about 2 tablespoons cream cheese. Spread 1 tablespoon of jelly over the cream cheese and sprinkle one-third of the pecans over the jelly. Roll each tortilla up tightly and wrap in plastic wrap. Refrigerate for at least 2 hours or overnight. When ready to serve, remove the plastic wrap and cut the rolls into ½-inch-thick slices. Arrange on a serving platter and serve.

Pepper Jelly

Makes 3 cups

½ cup finely chopped red bell pepper

½ cup finely chopped green bell pepper

¼ cup finely chopped jalapeño pepper

3 cups sugar

¾ cup cider vinegar

1 (3-ounce) package Certo liquid pectin

Stir together the peppers, sugar, and vinegar in a saucepan over medium-high heat. Bring to a boil, stirring, until the sugar is dissolved. Stir in the pectin and cook another 1 to 2 minutes. Remove from the heat. Let cool until slightly thickened, then ladle into sterilized jars (peppers will float to the top, so stir the mixture before transferring to the jars). Keep covered in the refrigerator for up to 3 months.

Mesquite Crêpes with Onion Filling and Leek Broth

Roxsand Scocos

Serves 12 as an appetizer

The beans of mesquite trees were a staple of Native Americans of the Sonoran Desert for centuries. Rich in sugar, they were dried on rooftops and ground into flour for making breads. Today, mesquite flour is available by mail order from Native Seeds/SEARCH in Tucson (see Mail-Order Sources, page 217). It gives these crêpes a unique, nutty flavor. Iitoi onions look and taste something like shallots; they've grown in the Southwest since the Spanish introduced them in the seventeenth century.

Crêpes

½ cup all-purpose flour

½ cup mesquite flour (substitute buckwheat flour)

3 eggs

1⅓ cups whole milk

1 tablespoon unsalted butter, melted

Filling

2 heads elephant garlic

2 tablespoons plus ½ cup olive oil

1 cup iitoi onion bulbs (substitute 1 cup Cipolline, Maui, or Walla Walla, cut into eighths)

8 red scallions (substitute green onions), green tops intact

Salt and freshly ground black pepper to taste

1 cup pearl onions, peeled

1 cup 1-inch pieces leeks (white part only)

2 cups white wine

2 tablespoons chopped marjoram or Greek oregano

For the crêpes: In a large bowl, whisk together all the ingredients. Allow to rest for 20 minutes. Heat a crêpe pan or 8-inch skillet over medium-high heat. Lightly coat the pan with butter or nonstick cooking spray. Add about 2 tablespoons of the batter to the hot pan and swirl the pan so the batter evenly coats the bottom. Put the pan back over the heat and cook the crêpe until the bottom side is lightly browned; flip over and cook the other side. Remove the crêpe to a plate. Repeat with the remaining batter until all is used. The crêpes can be made ahead, wrapped in plastic wrap, and refrigerated.

For the filling: Preheat the oven to 400°. Cut the tops (stem end) off the heads of garlic to expose the individual cloves. Place on a piece of aluminum foil and coat with 1 tablespoon olive oil. Wrap well and bake until tender, about 1 hour. Remove from the oven and squeeze the bulbs out onto a plate or into a bowl. Set aside.

Preheat a barbecue grill or broiler. Remove the green tops from the iitoi onion bulbs; reserve the bulbs and place the tops with the scallions or green onions (if not using iitoi onions, use 4 to 6 additional green onions). Drizzle with 1 tablespoon of the olive oil and season with salt and pepper to taste. Grill or broil the tops and scallions until lightly browned, 2 or 3 minutes. Remove from the heat, chop into ½-inch pieces, and set aside.

In a large, heavy-bottomed skillet over medium-high heat, place the remaining ½ cup olive oil. Add the onion bulbs, pearl onions, and salt and pepper to taste. Add the leeks and sauté quickly, about 1 minute (do not allow to brown). Reduce the heat to medium-low, cover the

Leek Broth

1 tablespoon olive oil

1 leek, white part only, washed well and finely chopped

½ cup dry white wine

1 tablespoon chopped marjoram or Greek oregano

2 cups chicken stock

4 tablespoons unsalted butter

Salt and freshly ground black pepper to taste

1½ cups crumbly cheese, such as queso cotija or asiago

Sprigs of fresh marjoram or Greek oregano, for garnish

pan, and cook until the onions are fork tender, 20 to 25 minutes. Remove the cover and add the grilled chopped scallions, roasted garlic cloves, white wine, and herbs. Raise the heat to high and cook until the liquid is gone, 25 to 30 minutes. Break the whole pearl onions with the back of a fork. The filling is now ready for the crêpes or can be refrigerated, covered, up to a day ahead of time.

For the leek broth: Heat the olive oil in a skillet over medium-high heat. Sauté the chopped leeks until tender, about 5 minutes. Add the white wine; raise the heat to high and cook until the pan is nearly dry, 3 to 5 minutes. Add the herbs and stock and cook until the liquid is reduced to about 1⅓ cups, another 10 minutes. Whisk in the butter. Strain and season with salt and pepper to taste; keep warm. The sauce will be quite thin, but will have a delicate leek flavor.

Assembly: Lay a crêpe out on a work surface. Spoon about ⅓ cup hot filling along the center of the crêpe and sprinkle 1 tablespoon crumbled or grated cheese on top of the filling; roll the crêpe into a cylinder around the filling and cheese and place on a serving plate. Spoon about 2 tablespoons of the broth around each filled crêpe; sprinkle another tablespoon of cheese over the crêpe and garnish with a sprig of herb. Repeat with the remaining crêpes and filling. Serve immediately.

 For onions, salt them when you first start to cook them. Salt draws out their moisture and brings up their sweetness. Be sure to cook the onions until they start to brown. Color equals flavor.

Onion Marmalade on Toasted Corn Bread

Makes about 32

White onions are preferred by many chefs in the Southwest for their sharpness and bite, a good foil to the many spicy ingredients they're paired with. Here, they cook down into a thick, syrupy preserve. The cayenne pepper supplies some unexpected heat.

Onion Marmalade

2 large white onions, thinly
  sliced
1½ cups chicken stock
1 tablespoon red wine vinegar
1 teaspoon salt
1 teaspoon cayenne pepper
½ teaspoon freshly ground black
  pepper
2 tablespoons heavy cream

1 loaf Green Chile Corn Bread
  (see Southwestern Corn
  Pudding, page 140)

Do Ahead { The marmalade can be made up to 2 days ahead, covered, and refrigerated. Bring back to room temperature before serving.

To make the onion marmalade: Place the onions in a heavy saucepan; add the stock, vinegar, salt, and peppers. Cover and cook over medium heat until the liquid has evaporated, about 30 minutes. Add the cream and bring the mixture to a boil. Cool to room temperature.

Assembly: Preheat a barbecue grill or broiler. Slice the bread into ¼-inch slices and grill or toast in the broiler on both sides until lightly browned. Halve diagonally and spread each triangle with a tablespoon of onion marmalade. Serve immediately.

 It's easiest to slice an onion if it lays flat. Halve the onion and set a half on the work surface, cut side down. With a sharp knife, slice it thinly into half moons and use as needed.

Cactus Rita

Jay McCarthy

Makes 5 or 6

When Jay began serving these magenta margaritas at Zuni Grill on San Antonio's River Walk in the early 1990s, the Texas Department of Agriculture called him to inquire why he needed half a ton of prickly pear fruit every two weeks! They recruited him to promote the prickly pear cactus to the rest of the world. He is now president of the Professional Association of Cactus Development.

6 prickly pear fruit (tunas), peeled
4 cups inexpensive tequila
½ cup freshly squeezed lime juice or undiluted Minute Maid frozen limeade
½ cup Triple Sec, Grand Marnier, or Cointreau
½ cup crushed ice
Honey or sugar syrup (optional)

Place the prickly pear fruit in a large glass container or jar. Top with tequila, cover, and refrigerate at least overnight or as long as 3 days. Transfer the prickly pears and tequila to a blender or food processor and purée. Strain through a sieve with holes large enough to hold back the seeds but let most of the pulp through. Measure out 1 cup of purée. Freeze the remainder for another use.

Place 1 cup purée, lime juice, liqueur, and ice in a blender; mix well. If it is too tart, add a little honey or sugar syrup. Pour into margarita glasses and serve immediately.

The peeled prickly pears soak in tequila for a two-way transfer of flavors that makes this cocktail extra delicious. The fruit can sit in the tequila up to 3 days before you use it. Extra purée freezes well.

Chapter

2

Salads

'Navajo Yellow' melon. 'Red Mustard' greens. 'Hopi Greasy Hair' corn. 'Zuni' tomatillo. 'Punta Banda' tomato. These remarkable heirloom vegetables grew in the Southwest a hundred years ago, but then disappeared from the modern table. But they've been returned to our markets with the support and enthusiasm of chefs like Tucson's Janos Wilder and such organizations as Native Seeds/SEARCH.

"Survival of the fittest" might best describe their timeless appeal. They are the edible form of seeds passed down from generation to generation as family treasures. Not always indigenous, they are natives nonetheless, selectively preserved over the years for their flavor, unique beauty, and above all for their amazing vitality despite marginal local conditions and frequent neglect. These hardy crops sustained the native peoples of the Southwest, but with migration, cultural changes, and environmental upheaval, many became scarce.

The revival of these living legacies of our agricultural past is the mission of the nonprofit Native Seeds/SEARCH of Tucson. Since its founding in 1983 in response to area Native Americans who sought to reestablish traditional crops, it has become a leader in the heirloom seed movement. With over 1,800 collections in its seed bank, it supplies farmers, home gardeners, and restaurant kitchens alike, with profits plowed back into operating funds.

That Janos Wilder opened his first Tucson restaurant in 1983 also may be more than serendipitous. Dedicated to locally grown, impeccably fresh ingredients, many from his own restaurant garden, Wilder soon became a vocal supporter of the organization, using their crops whenever possible. These long-forgotten foods appear on his menus in such tempting form as Blue Corn—Crusted Cabrilla with Rainbow Posole Broth (see page 112), made with heirloom red, blue, and white posole. Other Southwestern chefs were equally inspired by this newly available bounty. Phoenix's Roxsand Scocos stars them in her flavorful Anasazi Bean and Peruvian Potato Salad (see page 47).

You can taste the culinary heritage of the Southwest at restaurants like Janos, RoxSand, and others. Farmers' markets are another good source for the heirloom produce that gives today's Southwestern cooking a flavor at once old and new. But no matter where you live, seek out the best locally grown ingredients for the appetizing salads collected in this chapter. They give every dish a lively freshness and unique regional appeal that food grown elsewhere and shipped in can never have.

Chile Slaw

Donna Nordin

Serves 8 to 10

This brightly colored salad tastes as good as it looks, with a mix of flavors that dances in your mouth. Serve this slaw in place of the usual cabbage version at your next cookout. Jicama, sometimes called the Mexican potato, is sweet and nutty, with an appealing crunch. It's usually eaten raw in the Southwest.

Salad

3 poblano chiles, stemmed, seeded, and julienned in 2-inch lengths

2 red bell peppers, cored, seeded and julienned in 2-inch lengths

2 yellow bell peppers, cored, seeded, and julienned in 2-inch lengths

1 large or 2 small carrots, peeled and julienned in 2-inch lengths

1 medium jicama, peeled and julienned in 2-inch lengths

2 serrano chiles, cored, seeded, and finely diced

½ cup coarsely chopped cilantro leaves

Dressing

2 tomatoes, peeled and seeded

3 cloves garlic, finely chopped

½ teaspoon ground cumin

¾ cup sour cream

Salt and freshly ground black pepper to taste

Do Ahead The slaw, without the cilantro leaves, can be prepared a day ahead of time, covered, and refrigerated. Add the cilantro at least 15 minutes before serving.

Combine all salad ingredients in a large bowl.

For the dressing: In a blender or food processor, purée the tomatoes, garlic, cumin, and sour cream together. Season with salt and pepper to taste. Pour over vegetables and toss together. Make at least 15 minutes before serving so the flavors marry.

Green Bean and Corn Salad

Serves 6

This salad can be made year-round with frozen corn, but it's best when corn is in season. In a perfect world, you want to cook the corn as soon as it's picked from the field because the sugars quickly start to convert to starch. Try to buy corn from a farmers' market and use it the same day.

2 ears corn, blanched and kernels cut off the cob (about 2 cups kernels)

2 cups green beans, trimmed, blanched, and julienned

½ cup diced red bell pepper

¼ cup chopped black olives

¼ cup chopped red onion

1 tablespoon chopped fresh oregano

Salt and freshly ground black pepper to taste

¼ to ⅓ cup Poblano Buttermilk Dressing (see page 49)

Do Ahead { The salad can be made a day ahead without the fresh oregano, covered, and refrigerated. Add the oregano just before serving.

In a large bowl, toss together corn, green beans, bell pepper, olives, onion, and oregano. Season with salt and pepper to taste. Drizzle with ¼ cup of the dressing and mix well; taste and add more dressing, if desired. Serve cold or at room temperature.

Salad of Spring Melons and Green Onions

Robert McGrath

According to Robert, there's nothing better than sweet, ripe fruit to complement the flavor of golden-brown fried trout freshly caught from the stream. The acid of the fruit contrasts nicely with the richness of the fish. The ingredients are all portable, making the salad a good choice for a picnic. If you can't find chives, substitute the tops of green onions.

Robert serves this simple fruit salad with **Pan-Fried Canyon Trout (see page 113).**

2 cups diced watermelon
2 cups cantaloupe balls
2 cups diced honeydew melon
1 cup diagonally sliced green onions, white and light green parts
½ cup chopped chives (1-inch pieces)
¼ cup snipped garlic chives
1 cup raspberry vinegar

In a large bowl, combine all the salad ingredients and allow to sit for at least 1 hour so flavors blend.

Anasazi Bean and Peruvian Potato Salad

Roxsand Scocos   **Serves 8**

The subtle flavor of the lavender vinaigrette and the unique color of the potatoes makes this a truly memorable dish. Find Anasazi beans and purple potatoes at most specialty stores, some supermarkets, and by mail order (see Mail-Order Sources, page 217). Don't add tomatoes unless they are perfectly ripe. Note that the beans must soak overnight before you cook them.

Beans

1½ cups dried Anasazi beans or pinto beans
2 tablespoons olive oil
1 teaspoon salt
1 teaspoon freshly ground black pepper

Lavender Vinaigrette

¼ cup distilled white vinegar
1½ teaspoons lavender petals (available at health food stores)
1 shallot, unpeeled
1 large clove garlic, unpeeled
¾ cup plus 1 teaspoon olive oil
Salt and freshly ground black pepper to taste

Potatoes

1 tablespoon salt
1 tablespoon white vinegar
1½ pounds purple potatoes

2 ripe tomatoes, seeded and diced
4 cups mixed greens (watercress, mesclun, arugula, or lolla rossa)

Do Ahead } The beans and potatoes can be cooked a day ahead, covered, and refrigerated. The vinaigrette can be made a day ahead, covered, and refrigerated.

For the beans: Place the dried beans in a large pot and cover by 2 inches with water; refrigerate overnight. Drain and place the beans back in the pot with fresh water to cover by 2 inches (do not salt the water) over medium-high heat. Bring to a boil, then reduce the heat and simmer until the beans are tender but not broken or mushy, about 45 minutes. Drain and place in a large bowl. Toss in olive oil, salt, and pepper. Set aside.

For the vinaigrette: In a small saucepan over medium-high heat, bring the vinegar to a boil; remove from the heat and add the lavender. Cover and allow to stand for 1 hour; strain and discard the lavender. Preheat the oven to 350°. Put the shallot and garlic on a piece of aluminum foil and drizzle with 1 teaspoon of olive oil. Wrap tightly and bake until the garlic is soft, 30 to 45 minutes. Remove from the oven, unwrap, and squeeze the softened garlic and shallot from their skins into a blender or food processor. Add the strained vinegar and purée. With the machine running, slowly add the remaining ¾ cup of the olive oil until it is emulsified and smooth. Season with salt and pepper to taste and set aside.

For the potatoes: Bring a large pot of water to a boil over high heat. Add the salt and vinegar. Add the unpeeled potatoes (left whole if small and quartered if large), reduce the heat to low and cook until tender, about 20 to 30 minutes. Drain and let cool. Cut into ½-inch dice and add to the bowl with the cooked beans.

Assembly: Add the tomatoes and greens to the bowl with the beans and potatoes. Toss the ingredients very gently with the vinaigrette. Serve immediately.

Grilled Potato Salad

Serves 6

If you're grilling the main course, why not the salad? This simple, rustic mixture is thrown together from pantry staples. A chipotle-spiked mayonnaise gives it extra kick and roots it firmly in the Southwest.

2 pounds new potatoes, cleaned
Salt and freshly ground black
    pepper to taste
1 red onion, sliced into ½-inch
    slices
¼ cup diced red bell pepper
½ cup diced celery
½ cup Chipotle Mayonnaise (see
    page 204)

Do Ahead { The salad will keep, covered, in the refrigerator for up to 2 days.

Bring a large pot of water to a boil over high heat; add the potatoes and cook until just tender, 15 to 20 minutes. Remove from the heat. Drain and cut into halves or quarters, depending on the size of the potatoes. Season with salt and pepper to taste.

Prepare a barbecue grill. When hot, place the potatoes and onion slices on the grill. Cook until lightly brown on one side, about 5 minutes. Carefully turn over and cook until caramelized, about another 5 minutes.

Place the grilled potatoes and onions in a large bowl. Add the bell pepper and celery. Add chipotle mayonnaise and toss well. Season with salt and pepper to taste.

Browning the onion and the potatoes on the grill gives them a sweeter, more complex flavor that's well worth the few extra minutes of cooking time.

Greens with Poblano Buttermilk Dressing and Corn Bread Croutons

Serves 6

Leftover corn bread becomes something altogether new when cut up into croutons. Float them in a soup or toss the toasted cubes in a tasty salad like this one. There's chile in the corn bread and in the dressing, but creamy buttermilk, mayonnaise, and avocado soothe away the heat.

Dressing

1 poblano chile, roasted, peeled, and seeded
¼ cup buttermilk
¼ cup mayonnaise
1 tablespoon chopped green onion
1 clove garlic, chopped
1 teaspoon freshly squeezed lime juice
1 teaspoon finely chopped cilantro
Salt and freshly ground black pepper to taste

½ loaf Green Chile Corn Bread (see page 154), cut into ½-inch cubes
8 to 10 cups mixed greens (arugula, red leaf, mesclun, romaine, frisee, endive, etc.)
1 cup diced red or yellow bell pepper
2 avocados, peeled, pitted, and thinly sliced

Do Ahead { The dressing can be made up to 1 week ahead, covered, and refrigerated. Croutons can be made up to 2 days ahead and kept in an airtight container.

For the dressing: Place all the dressing ingredients into a blender and purée. Set aside.

Preheat the oven to 350°. Place the corn bread cubes on a baking sheet and toast in a preheated oven until lightly browned, about 10 minutes.

In a large bowl, toss together the greens and bell pepper. Toss with just enough dressing to coat the greens. Divide evenly among 6 plates; arrange the avocado and corn bread croutons on top. Serve immediately.

Romaine with Tortillas and Piquant Citrus Dressing

Serves 8

This great Southwestern salad works with any sort of meal. The tortillas are crisped in the oven instead of fried: They're lightly sprayed with oil, sprinkled with chile powder, and baked. The result is much healthier than the usual chips, and just as delicious. The dressing is best made at least a few hours ahead of time so the flavors blend well.

Dressing

1 canned chipotle chile in adobo sauce, finely chopped

3 tablespoons freshly squeezed orange juice

1 tablespoon freshly squeezed lime juice

1 tablespoon finely chopped cilantro

1 teaspoon cumin seed, toasted and ground

Salt and freshly ground black pepper to taste

1/3 cup olive oil

Tortillas

3 flour tortillas, 8 inches in diameter

Nonstick cooking spray or olive oil

1 tablespoon chile powder

8 to 10 cups torn romaine lettuce leaves (about 1 large head)

1 large ripe tomato, seeded and diced

1 cup crumbled cotija cheese or queso fresco or other mild cheese

Do Ahead { The dressing can be made up to 2 days ahead, covered, and refrigerated. The tortillas can be baked a day ahead and kept in an airtight container.

For the dressing: In a small bowl, whisk together the chipotle, juices, cilantro, cumin, salt, and pepper. Gradually add the olive oil; adjust the seasonings to taste and set aside.

For the tortillas: Preheat the oven to 350°. With a sharp knife, cut the tortillas into 2 x ¼-inch strips. Place on a baking sheet and spray lightly with nonstick cooking spray or olive oil. Sprinkle with chile powder. Bake until the tortillas are slightly browned, 5 to 7 minutes. Remove from the oven and let cool.

Assembly: In a large bowl, combine the lettuce, tomato, and cheese. Toss in just enough dressing to moisten the ingredients and divide the mixture among 8 salad plates. Sprinkle the tortilla slices over the greens and serve immediately.

Fiesta Chicken Salad

Serves 4

On a balmy summer's night, this quick and tasty main-course salad is a perfect light supper to serve outdoors. A good loaf of bread and a glass of wine is all the company it needs, followed by sweet, fresh fruit for dessert. As a shortcut, substitute purchased smoked chicken or turkey breast (you'll need about 1½ pounds) for the grilled chicken breasts.

4 boneless, skinless chicken breast halves

2 teaspoons freshly squeezed lemon juice

Salt and freshly ground black pepper to taste

1 cup diced yellow bell pepper

1 cup seeded and diced ripe tomato

1 cup jicama, peeled and julienned

½ cup diced red onion

¾ cup Chipotle Mayonnaise (see page 204)

8 cups mixed salad greens

Sprinkle the chicken breasts with lemon juice, salt and pepper. Cook the chicken breasts on the grill using wood chips or in a smoker for about 15 to 20 minutes, until just cooked through (about 180° internal temperature). Dice the chicken (there should be about 5 cups) and place into a large bowl. Add the bell pepper, tomato, jicama, and red onion. Add the chipotle mayonnaise and toss well.

Arrange the greens on the bottom of 4 large plates or shallow bowls. Top the greens with the chicken mixture. Serve immediately.

To give lettuce crunch and to keep it fresh for days, wash greens in a sink of cold water mixed with 1 tablespoon sugar and 1 tablespoon white vinegar. Then spin the lettuce dry and store in unsealed plastic bags, layered with paper towels.

Margarita Shrimp Salad

Every amateur mixologist in the Southwest claims to know the secret to the perfect margarita, the region's popular cocktail made with tequila, Triple Sec, and lime juice. Test their margarita IQ with this spirited shrimp salad to see if they can identify the basics in the dressing. It's a dynamite first course or centerpiece of a summer dinner.

Shrimp

2 tablespoons chopped cilantro

2 cloves garlic, minced

1 serrano chile, stemmed, seeded, and finely diced

⅓ cup tequila

2 tablespoons Triple Sec or Grand Marnier

¼ cup freshly squeezed lime juice

1 teaspoon cumin seed, toasted and ground, or 1 teaspoon ground cumin

1 pound shrimp (16 to 20 per pound), peeled, deveined, and slit open along the backs

¼ cup olive oil

Salt and freshly ground black pepper to taste

Salad

4 corn tortillas, 6 inches in diameter, cut into julienne

Vegetable oil for frying tortillas

1 teaspoon chile powder

1 tomato, cored, seeded, and diced

1 yellow bell pepper, cored, seeded, and diced

6 cups torn romaine lettuce leaves, washed and thoroughly dried

For the shrimp: Combine the cilantro, garlic, chile, tequila, Triple Sec, lime juice, and cumin seed in a nonreactive bowl. Add the shrimp, turn to coat, and refrigerate for at least 1 hour. Drain the shrimp and reserve the marinade.

In a small saucepan over high heat, bring the reserved marinade to a boil. Reduce the heat to medium and simmer until reduced by half. Remove from the heat, transfer to a bowl, and let cool. Whisk in the olive oil and season with salt and pepper to taste. Set aside.

Prepare a barbecue grill or preheat a broiler. Grill or broil the shrimp until just pink, about 1 minute per side. Keep warm.

For the salad: Fill a small skillet with oil to a depth of about 1 inch and place over medium heat. When the oil is about 375°, fry the tortilla strips in batches until light brown and crisp. Drain on paper towels. Sprinkle with chile powder while still warm.

In a large bowl, mix together the tomato, bell pepper, and lettuce. Toss with the marinade-oil dressing and divide among 4 large plates or shallow bowls. Top the salad with grilled shrimp and fried tortilla strips. Serve immediately.

Red Chile Pasta Salad

Serves 8 to 10

With a pasta machine, making your own pasta is fun, gratifying, and easy. If you lack the time to make it—or the inclination—use your favorite prepared fresh or dry fettucine. Piñon nuts are prized by the Navajo and the Hopi peoples, who gather them during the winter. Yields vary from year to year, so these nuts are not always readily available. If you can't find them, substitute easy-to-find pine nuts.

Red Chili Pasta

1 cup unbleached all-purpose flour
½ cup semolina flour
3 tablespoons chile powder
½ teaspoon ground cumin
1 teaspoon salt
2 large eggs
1 tablespoon olive oil

Dressing

1 clove garlic, peeled and finely chopped
1 tablespoon finely chopped cilantro
1 tablespoon white wine vinegar
2 tablespoons freshly squeezed orange juice
¼ teaspoon salt
⅛ teaspoon cayenne pepper
1 ½ teaspoons dry mustard
½ cup olive oil

Salad

12 spinach leaves, stemmed
⅓ cup shelled piñon nuts, toasted (substitute pine nuts)
1 zucchini, coarsely grated
8 ounces goat cheese such as Montrachet
4 tomatoes, seeded and diced

Do Ahead { The cooked pasta can be tossed with ½ cup of the dressing up to 1 day ahead. Cover and refrigerate.

For the pasta: Using a food processor fitted with the metal blade, combine the flours and seasonings. Then add the eggs and oil and process to make a smooth ball, adding flour or water as needed. Knead in the processor for 60 seconds. Wrap the dough in plastic wrap and let it rest for 20 minutes in the refrigerator. Process the dough through a pasta machine, using the fettucine cutter. Cook the pasta in boiling, salted water until al dente, 3 to 4 minutes. Rinse and set aside.

For the dressing: Whisk together the garlic, cilantro, vinegar, orange juice, salt, cayenne, and mustard. Whisk in the oil, beating until the dressing is thick and smooth. Set aside.

For the salad: In a large bowl, toss ½ cup of the dressing with the pasta; set aside.

Stack up the cleaned spinach leaves, roll up into a cylinder and cut into strips (a chiffonade). Add the toasted piñon nuts, zucchini, and cut spinach leaves to the pasta; toss well. Crumble the goat cheese over the pasta mixture; sprinkle tomatoes over all. Just before serving, mix well. Serve immediately and pass extra dressing.

 To peel a clove of garlic, whack it with the side of a chef's knife. If you first moisten the blade a bit with a little water, the garlic is less likely to stick to it.

Nopales, Jicama, and Orange Salad

Serves 4 to 6

Nopales are the pads of the prickly pear cactus and are sold in supermarkets throughout the Southwest. Fresh pads need to be peeled, cut into strips, and briefly blanched in boiling water. Prepared pads are sold in jars in Latino markets and some supermarkets. Rinse and drain them before using.

1 cup julienned nopales (if using from a jar, rinse well and drain)
1 cup julienned jicama
2 navel oranges, peeled and sectioned
1 tablespoon pepitas (pumpkin seeds), toasted
1 tablespoon grated orange zest
1 tablespoon freshly squeezed orange juice
1 tablespoon olive oil
Salt and freshly ground black pepper to taste

Do Ahead { The salad can be made without the pepitas a day ahead, covered, and refrigerated. Add the pepitas just before serving.

Toss the nopales, jicama, oranges, pepitas, and zest together in a nonreactive bowl. Whisk the orange juice and olive oil together in a small bowl; stir into the salad. Season with salt and pepper to taste. Serve at room temperature.

Chapter 3

Soups, Stews, and Chilis

Long before Columbus or the Pilgrims, or even before the Crusades, the holy trinity of corn, squash, and beans was being cultivated throughout the Americas. So important were these three foods to Native Americans that they spoke of them as the Three Sisters and planted them together in natural synergy: The corn supports the beans, which in turn restores nitrogen to the soil depleted by the corn. The squash, too, supplies important nutrients.

Almost every nation tells the legend, says chef Loretta Barrett Oden. Her favorite version follows on the next page. Oden, an Oklahoma Potawatomi, serves the Three Sisters and many other indigenous New World foods at her Corn Dance Cafe in Santa Fe, New Mexico.

The restaurant's name reflects the reverence that the native peoples of the Southwest have

for food, and for corn in particular. Corn dance ceremonies offer thanks for a bountiful harvest and pray for rain for the next year's crops. Some tribes even hold that their bodies are made of corn, which they consider a sacred gift from the gods. Tiny grains of corn pollen are placed in Navajo sand paintings to cure the sick, and they appear as body paint in ceremonial dances. Among the Pueblo Indians, the colors of corn represent directions—white is east, blue is west, yellow is north, and red is south.

Corn not only played a large part in the development of indigenous tribes, but also in the survival of Europeans who settled here. The Pilgrims probably couldn't have established their colony without learning its cultivation, in concert with squash and beans, from friendly tribes. It's one of the New World's greatest gifts to the Old.

Corn, squash, and beans—plus the many other native foods of the Southwest, from chiles to tomatoes—combine in the robust, spirit-satisfying bowls in this chapter. In honor of the Three Sisters, why not start with Three Sisters Stew with Corn Dumplings (see page 66), Loretta Barrett Oden's culinary homage to her Native American heritage.

There were three young girls of the same tribe, from different clans, but close enough to be sisters. On the last evening before the tribe split up to go to the winter hunting grounds, the sisters went out to play. "How can we stay together?" they wondered. The next morning they were gone. But, in the field their parents found a very tall stalk of corn. This was the strong sister. A bean vine twined up around it. This was the shy sister. Down below, a squash plant grew, smothering out the weeds and holding in the moisture. This was the earthy, funny sister. So, the Three Sisters had found a way to stay together.

Roasted Acorn Squash Soup

Donna Nordin   **Serves 8**

Squash is one of the oldest of the indigenous foods of the Americas, with special significance to Native Americans. This full-flavored soup would dispel the chill on a crisp autumn evening. Because it uses low-fat milk and sour cream, it is a healthy alternative to other cream soups.

2 acorn squash, halved and
  seeded
1 tablespoon vegetable oil
¼ cup diced roasted yellow bell
  pepper
¼ cup thinly sliced carrots
½ cup thinly sliced onion
1 teaspoon finely chopped garlic
6 cups water
1 teaspoon chopped fresh thyme
1 tablespoon chopped fresh basil
¼ teaspoon ground cinnamon
¼ teaspoon ground allspice
¼ teaspoon freshly grated
  nutmeg
2 tablespoons brown sugar
Salt and freshly ground black
  pepper to taste
½ cup low-fat milk
½ cup low-fat sour cream, for
  garnish
½ teaspoon puréed chipotle chile
  in adobo sauce, or
  1 teaspoon chile powder, for
  garnish
6 green onions, white and light
  green parts, thinly sliced, for
  garnish

Preheat the oven to 350°. Place the squash halves on a baking sheet and roast until soft, about 1 hour. Cool.

In a large saucepan or Dutch oven, heat the vegetable oil over medium heat. Add the yellow pepper, carrots, onion, and garlic; cook until soft, 5 to 10 minutes. Scoop the pulp from the squash and add to the pan along with the water. Stir and simmer for 30 minutes. Purée the mixture in a food processor or blender and return to the pan. Stir in herbs and spices. Add the milk and adjust the seasonings to taste. Heat over medium heat until the soup is hot.

Combine the sour cream and chipotle purée in a squeeze bottle or small bowl. Shake or whisk until well blended.

Ladle soup into 8 bowls. Garnish each with a "squiggle" of chipotle cream (from the squeeze bottle or by drizzling in a thin stream with a spoon) and a tablespoon of sliced green onions.

Tricolor Soup

Donna Nordin
Serves 6

The secret to the presentation of this delicious soup is to have all three elements the same consistency so they don't sink into one another. The result is stunning.

Soup Base

1 tablespoon olive oil
½ cup chopped white onion
¼ cup chopped yellow onion
2 green onions, chopped
1 shallot, chopped
1 clove garlic, chopped
1 serrano chile, chopped
½ cup white wine
1½ cups water
1½ cups heavy cream
½ teaspoon salt

White Bean Soup

1 cup dried white beans
4 cups water
½ teaspoon salt
½ cup water, if needed

Squash Soup

1 butternut squash
¼ teaspoon ground cinnamon
¼ teaspoon ground allspice
¼ teaspoon salt
½ cup water, if needed

Roasted Garlic–Green Onion Purée

½ cup roasted garlic (3 heads)
1 cup chopped green onions
1 small jalapeño, stemmed, seeded, and chopped
¼ cup chopped parsley
2 tablespoons olive oil
½ cup water, if needed
Salt to taste

Do Ahead { The soup base can be made ahead, covered, and refrigerated for up to 2 days.

For the soup base: In a skillet over high heat, heat the olive oil. When hot, reduce the heat to medium and add the onions, garlic, and chile. Sauté until the vegetables are softened, about 5 minutes. Add the wine, water, and cream and bring to a boil. Simmer for 10 minutes. Put the mixture in a blender and purée. Add salt to taste and set aside.

For the white bean soup: Place the beans, water, and salt in a large saucepan over high heat; bring to a boil. Reduce the heat to low and simmer until the beans are soft and slightly "overcooked," about 1 hour. Strain the beans and let cool. Place the beans and 2 cups of the soup base in a blender and purée. Thin with water, if necessary, to achieve the desired consistency.

For the squash soup: Preheat an oven to 400°. Halve the squash end to end and scoop out the seeds. Place the squash on a baking sheet and bake until soft, 45 to 60 minutes. Let cool. Scoop the flesh out of the skin into a 2-cup measuring cup. Place 1½ cups of the squash in a blender with the cinnamon, allspice, salt, and 2 cups of the soup base. Purée until smooth and add water, if necessary, to achieve the desired consistency.

For the garlic-onion purée: Place the garlic, onions, jalapeño, parsley, and oil in a blender and purée until smooth. Add salt to taste and add water, if necessary, to achieve the desired consistency.

To serve, heat both soups and adjust the water content so they are both the same consistency. Ladle both soups at the same time into each soup bowl. Give the bowl a slight spin for a swirled effect. Squiggle a design with the garlic-onion purée over the two soups with a plastic squeeze bottle or with a spoon. Serve immediately.

Pumpkin Soup with Toasted Pepitas

Serves 4 to 6

Since pre-Columbian times, New World cooks were making sauces with pepitas (pumpkin seeds), and also fired up their food with the chiltepín, a hot red chile that looks like a berry and still grows wild in much of the Southwest. If you can't find the wild chile for this autumnal soup, the cultivated variety, pequin, can substitute.

2 tablespoons unsalted butter
1 cup finely chopped onion
   (2 large onions)
1 chiltepín, crushed
¼ teaspoon cayenne pepper
1½ cups cooked pumpkin (fresh
   or canned)
1 teaspoon salt
⅔ cup milk
2 cups chicken stock
¼ cup raw hulled pepitas
   (pumpkin seeds), for garnish

Do Ahead { The soup can be made up to 2 days ahead, covered, and refrigerated. Bring to a simmer just before serving. Pepitas can be toasted up to 2 days ahead and stored in an airtight container.

Melt the butter in a large skillet over medium heat. Add the onion and sauté until soft and translucent, 5 to 10 minutes. Add the chiltepín and cayenne pepper. Place the onion mixture in a blender or food processor with the pumpkin, salt, and milk; purée until smooth. Pour mixture into a large saucepan, add the chicken stock and bring to a boil. Reduce the heat and simmer until the soup is hot and the ingredients are well incorporated, 10 to 15 minutes.

Place the raw pepitas in a large nonstick skillet and toast over medium heat, stirring, until the seeds are fragrant, light brown, and begin to pop, 2 to 3 minutes. Set aside.

To serve, ladle the soup into bowls. Sprinkle about 1 tablespoon of toasted pepitas on top of each serving.

Toasting deepens the flavor of any seed, pepitas included.

Creamy Carrot Soup

In this tasty soup, the sweetness of the carrots is set off by the unexpected heat of a jalapeño chile. The lime-infused garnish could be drizzled on with a spoon, but applying it with a squeeze bottle—a favorite in professional kitchens—lets you explore your artistic potential. The plastic bottles with pointed tips are available in supermarkets and hardware stores.

6 tablespoons unsalted butter

2 cups coarsely chopped onions

1 tablespoon finely chopped garlic

1½ pounds carrots (about 6 large), peeled and sliced

2 cups chopped tomatoes (canned, with the juices, may be used)

¼ teaspoon ground allspice

¼ cup chopped cilantro

1 red jalapeño chile (also called Fresno red chile), finely chopped

6 cups chicken stock

½ cup heavy cream

⅓ cup freshly squeezed orange juice

Salt and freshly ground black pepper to taste

Mexican Cream, for garnish (see page 203)

Do Ahead { The soup can be made up to 2 days ahead, covered, and refrigerated, but don't add the orange juice, salt, and pepper until just before serving. When ready to serve, bring to a simmer and stir in the juice, salt, and pepper.

In a large saucepan, melt the butter over medium heat. Add the onions and garlic and sauté until translucent, about 5 minutes. Add the carrots, tomatoes, allspice, cilantro, jalapeño, and stock. Bring to a boil over high heat; cover, reduce the heat to low, and simmer for 1 hour. Strain, reserving liquid. Purée the vegetables in a food processor until smooth. Return the reserved liquid and puréed vegetables to the pan and add the cream. Simmer for 15 minutes. Stir in the orange juice and season with salt and pepper to taste.

Ladle the soup into bowls. Drizzle designs with the Mexican cream on top in a thin stream with a plastic squeeze bottle or a spoon.

Smoky Fideo Soup

Mary Sue Milliken and Susan Feniger

The chefs' earthy, smoky chipotle sauce gives this soup its deep, complex flavor. The sauce can be made ahead and refrigerated for several days or frozen, leaving little to do at the last minute.

3 tablespoons olive oil

8 ounces fideo, vermicelli, or angel hair pasta, broken into 1-inch pieces

1 cup diced onion

1 teaspoon salt

4 cloves garlic, minced

4 plum tomatoes, cored, seeded, and diced

1 cup Chipotle Sauce (see page 194)

4 cups chicken or vegetable stock

1 small avocado, peeled, seeded, and cut into 8 slices, for garnish

½ cup chopped cilantro leaves, for garnish

8 lime wedges, for garnish

Heat the olive oil in a large saucepan over medium-low heat. Add the pasta and sauté, stirring frequently, until light golden brown, about 5 minutes. Stir in the onion and salt, and cook until the onion is slightly golden, 5 minutes longer. Add the garlic and cook another minute to release the aromas. Add the tomatoes, chipotle sauce, and stock. Bring to a boil; reduce the heat to medium-low and simmer until the noodles soften and the flavors meld, about 15 minutes. Divide into 8 soup bowls and garnish each with a slice of avocado, a tablespoon of cilantro leaves, and a lime wedge.

The fat of the avocado absorbs the heat of the chiles, so its creaminess evens out their spice.

Southwestern Vegetable Soup

Serves 6

Not plain chicken soup, but chile soup is the comfort food that Southwesterners turn to when they're not feeling up to par. Capsaicin, the compound that gives chiles their heat, is a proven germ-killer. For a vegetarian meal, use vegetable stock and eliminate the cheese.

2 large ripe tomatoes, halved horizontally

5 cups vegetable or chicken stock

1 tablespoon olive oil

2 cups diced white onions (2 large)

1 jalapeño chile, stemmed, seeded, and finely chopped

2 cloves garlic, finely chopped

½ cup amber beer, such as Dos Equis

5 long green chiles, roasted, peeled, seeded, and diced

2 cups peeled and diced Idaho potato (1 large)

1 tablespoon freshly squeezed lime juice

1 tablespoon Achiote Paste (see page 205)

1 tablespoon sugar

Salt and freshly ground black pepper to taste

½ cup finely chopped cilantro

½ cup crumbled tangy white cheese, such as cotija or queso fresco

Preheat a broiler. Arrange the tomato halves, cut side down, on a baking sheet. Broil until the skins are charred, about 5 minutes. Transfer the tomatoes to a nonreactive saucepan, add the stock, and bring to a boil over high heat. Reduce the heat to low and simmer for 20 minutes. Strain the mixture into a large bowl, pressing on the solids with a rubber spatula to extract all the juices.

In a large nonreactive saucepan, heat the olive oil over medium heat. Add the onions, jalapeño, and garlic. Cook, stirring occasionally, until the onions are softened, about 5 minutes. Add the beer, raise the heat to high, and bring to a boil; boil for 3 minutes. Add the strained stock, roasted chiles, potato, lime juice, achiote paste, and sugar. Reduce the heat to medium; simmer until the potatoes are tender, about 20 minutes. Season with salt and pepper to taste. Stir in the chopped cilantro. Ladle the soup into shallow bowls and sprinkle with cheese.

Three Sisters Stew with Corn Dumplings

Loretta Barrett Oden

Serves 8

Traditionally, Native Americans grow corn, squash, and beans—the Three Sisters—together in mounds as garden companions. The beans and squash actually replace nutrients in the soil that the corn depletes, while the corn stalk acts as a natural trellis for the bean vine.

½ cup dried Anasazi beans or pinto beans
½ cup dried lima beans
½ cup dried white beans
½ cup dried black beans
1 tablespoon olive oil
1½ cups finely chopped yellow onion
1½ cups finely chopped green bell pepper
2 tablespoons finely chopped garlic
1 jalapeño chile, stemmed, seeded, and finely chopped
2 teaspoons cumin seed
⅛ teaspoon cayenne pepper
2 teaspoons chile powder
1 (28-ounce) can peeled tomatoes, with juice
3 quarts water
3 ears corn (about 3 cups corn kernels)
½ cup beer
2 cups diced zucchini, yellow squash, and/or other summer squash

Dumplings

½ cup yellow cornmeal
½ cup all-purpose flour
2 teaspoons baking powder
½ teaspoon salt
½ teaspoon sugar
1 egg
⅓ cup milk
1 tablespoon unsalted butter, melted
½ cup cooked fresh, thawed frozen, or drained canned corn kernels

Place the beans in a large saucepan or Dutch oven. Cover with water by 2 inches and soak 2 hours or overnight. Drain and set aside.

Heat the olive oil in a large saucepan or Dutch oven over medium-high heat; sauté the onions, bell pepper, garlic, and jalapeño until soft, about 5 minutes. In a dry small skillet, toast the cumin seed until aromatic and lightly browned; grind in a mini food processor or coffee or spice grinder, and add to the onion mixture. In the same skillet, toast the cayenne and chile powder for just 1 or 2 minutes, being careful not to burn; add to the onion mixture. Add the tomatoes to the onion mixture and simmer for 15 minutes. Add the 3 quarts water and drained beans to the pan and bring to a boil. Reduce the heat and simmer until the beans are tender, about 1½ to 2 hours. Cut the corn kernels off the cob. Add the beer, corn kernels, and squash and cook until the squash is tender, about 10 minutes. Add salt and pepper to taste.

For the dumplings: In a bowl, stir together the cornmeal, flour, baking powder, salt, and sugar. In another bowl or glass measuring cup, whisk together the egg, milk, and butter. Add the liquid mixture to the dry and mix just until incorporated; fold in the corn. Drop the batter by heaping tablespoons into the slowly simmering stew (there should be about 16 dumplings). Cover and cook until a wooden toothpick inserted into the centers of the dumplings comes out clean, about 15 minutes.

Spoon the stew into bowls and top each serving with 2 dumplings. Serve immediately.

You don't have to soak beans overnight. To quick-soak: Pick and sort the beans, then cover with cold water. Bring to a boil, cover the pot, and remove it from the heat. Let sit 1 hour. Drain off the soaking liquid and fill the pot with fresh water. Cook as directed.

Seafood Stew

Fish transported to our markets gives Southwestern cooks who love seafood many choices. Claimed as our own is talapia, a mild white fish farm-raised in southern Arizona as part of an aquaculture program of the University of Arizona.

6 cups fish stock or clam juice

2 tablespoons freshly squeezed lime juice

¼ cup Red Sauce (see page 197) or Chipotle Sauce (see page 194)

1 teaspoon salt

1 pound shrimp (26 to 30 per pound), unpeeled

1 tablespoon olive oil

1 cup finely chopped onion

1 tablespoon finely chopped garlic

1 tablespoon finely chopped oregano, or 1 teaspoon dried

1 cup seeded and diced tomato

1 poblano chile, roasted, seeded, peeled, and diced

1 cup corn kernels

1 pound halibut or talapia fillet, cut into 1-inch pieces

Salt and freshly ground black pepper to taste

Combine the stock, 1 tablespoon of the lime juice, sauce, and salt in a large saucepan over medium-high heat. Bring to a boil, add the shrimp, and cook until the shrimp just turn pink, about 2 minutes. Remove the shrimp with a slotted spoon; reduce the heat and keep the stock at a low simmer. Peel and devein the shrimp, discard the shells, and set the shrimp aside.

In a large skillet, heat the olive oil over medium heat. When hot, add the onion and the garlic, and cook until the vegetables are tender, about 5 minutes. Add the oregano and cook 1 minute more. Stir in the tomato, diced chile, and corn. Cook, stirring until the corn is tender, about 5 minutes.

Spoon the onion mixture into the hot stock and add the fish pieces. Cook, stirring occasionally, until the fish is cooked through, about 5 minutes. Add the shrimp and cook until warmed through, another 1 to 2 minutes. Add the remaining tablespoon lime juice and salt and pepper to taste. Ladle into 6 shallow bowls and serve immediately.

 If you use dried oregano rather than fresh, rub it between your hands before adding it to the stew. This action releases its essential oils and makes it more flavorful.

Golden Gazpacho with Rock Shrimp Salsa

Chuck Wiley

Serves 4

Spain takes the credit for inventing this cold fresh tomato soup, but the Southwest—and Chuck Wiley—claims this version made with bright yellow tomatoes instead of the usual red ones. Perhaps this is the gold the Spanish sought in the Southwest centuries ago!

Gazpacho

1 pound golden tomatoes (about 3 medium), cored and quartered

1 cucumber (about 8 ounces), peeled, seeded, and coarsely chopped

1 yellow bell pepper, cored, seeded, and coarsely chopped

1 serrano chile, halved, seeds and veins removed

¼ cup vegetable stock

2 tablespoons rice wine vinegar

Salt and freshly ground black pepper to taste

Salsa

1 teaspoon olive oil

6 ounces rock shrimp, rinsed and deveined (substitute gulf shrimp, cut in bite-sized pieces)

1 clove garlic, finely chopped

½ cup finely chopped red onion

1 small yellow bell pepper, cored, seeded, and finely chopped (about ½ cup)

1 small red bell pepper, cored, seeded, and finely chopped (about ½ cup)

1 cup cored, seeded, and diced tomato

1 tablespoon freshly squeezed lime juice

2 teaspoons chopped cilantro

Salt and freshly ground black pepper to taste

Do Ahead { The gazpacho can be made up to 2 days ahead, covered, and refrigerated.

For the gazpacho: Place all gazpacho ingredients in a blender; purée until smooth. Strain through a large-holed sieve into a bowl, cover, and refrigerate.

For the salsa: Heat the olive oil in an 8-inch skillet over medium heat. Add the shrimp and cook until they turn pink and lose their translucency, 3 to 4 minutes. Add the garlic and cook 1 minute more. Turn out into a bowl and let cool. When cool, add the onion, peppers, tomato, lime juice, and cilantro. Mix well and season with salt and pepper to taste.

Assembly: Divide gazpacho among 4 chilled bowls. Place about ½ cup salsa in the center of each bowl. Serve immediately.

Chilled Tomato Soup with Cilantro Crème Fraîche

Serves 6

This flavor-packed soup uses canned tomatoes and produce staples, and assembles in minutes, making it ideal fare for spur-of-the-moment entertaining. The soup and the crème fraîche must be the same consistency, so adjust accordingly.

Soup

- 4 cloves garlic, peeled
- 4 slices stale white bread, crusts removed
- 1 tablespoon red wine vinegar
- 1 tablespoon sugar
- ¼ cup olive oil
- 1 (28-ounce) can plum tomatoes, with juice
- 2 cups tomato juice
- 6 green onions, white and light green parts, finely chopped
- 1 cucumber, peeled, seeded, and chopped
- 2 red bell peppers, roasted, peeled, seeded, and chopped
- 2 tablespoons fresh basil, chopped
- Salt and freshly ground black pepper to taste

Cilantro Crème Fraîche:

- 2 cups water
- 8 spinach leaves
- 1 cup loosely packed fresh cilantro leaves
- 3 tablespoons milk
- 2 tablespoons crème fraîche (made by combining 1 tablespoon of buttermilk with 1 cup of whipping cream in a covered jar and allowing to sit at room temperature until thick, about 24 hours)

For the soup: With the food processor running, add the cloves of garlic through the feed tube into the work bowl. Turn off the machine and crumble the bread into the work bowl. Add the vinegar and blend, then add the sugar and blend again. With the processor running, slowly add as much olive oil as the bread will absorb without becoming oily. Add the tomatoes, tomato juice, green onions, cucumber, red peppers, and chopped basil. Purée. Turn out into a large bowl; if the consistency is too thick, add more tomato juice. Season with salt and pepper to taste. Refrigerate for at least 2 hours and up to 2 days.

For the cilantro crème fraîche: Bring the water to a boil in a small saucepan. Add the spinach and boil 1 minute; drain. Plunge the spinach into ice water to stop the cooking; drain and squeeze dry. Transfer the spinach to a blender. Add the cilantro and milk and purée thoroughly. Strain the mixture through a fine sieve into a bowl. Whisk in the crème fraîche. Cover and chill until ready to use. If it is thinner than the soup, add more crème fraîche; if thicker, add more milk.

To serve, ladle the soup into 6 cold bowls. Drizzle with cilantro crème fraîche.

 To trim leaves from cilantro, give it a "haircut": Lay the bunch on its side on a cutting board: Holding the stems in your hand, slide a sharp chef's knife down the stems; the leaves will fall to the board.

Traditional Posole

Serves 6

The original Southwest comfort food, posole is an ancient feast day dish. It's a favorite on New Year's Day, eaten for good luck (just like black-eyed peas are in the South). You can't find a better choice for entertaining: it's simple, can be made ahead, and stays warm for hours on the stove while your guests help themselves. It's made with hominy, a lime-slaked corn that in the Southwest is also called posole. If you use dried hominy instead of canned, soak it overnight in water. (Pictured right, with Chili con Carne, recipe page 74)

2 dried red New Mexico chiles, stemmed and seeded

1 teaspoon cumin seed

3 cups canned hominy, rinsed and drained

1½ pounds lean boneless pork, cut into ½-inch cubes

2 cups finely chopped white onion

1 tablespoon finely chopped garlic

1 teaspoon dried oregano

6 cups water

2 teaspoons salt

Red Sauce (see page 197), Ancho Chile Relish (see page 209), or Chipotle Sauce (see page 194), for accompaniment

Heat a large, heavy-bottomed saucepan or Dutch oven over medium heat. When hot, add the chiles and toast until slightly softened and aromatic, about 1 minute per side. Remove from the pan and tear into small pieces; set aside. In the same pan, add the cumin seed and toast until lightly browned and aromatic, 1 to 2 minutes. Transfer to a coffee or spice grinder, mini food processor, or a mortar and pestle and crush the seeds; set aside.

Combine the hominy, pork, onions, garlic, oregano, water, chile pieces, cumin seed, and 1 teaspoon of the salt in the pan. Bring to a boil over high heat; reduce the heat and simmer, uncovered, until the meat is tender and the kernels of hominy burst and are swelled, 2 to 2½ hours. The stew should have plenty of liquid, so add more water if necessary throughout the cooking time. Taste for salt and add the remaining teaspoon salt, if necessary. Serve with the sauces of your choice.

 This is a rustic stew, so you don't need to crush the toasted cumin seed to a powder. To prepare the dried chiles, just pull off the stem, shake out the seeds, and tear into strips.

Anasazi Chili

The Anasazi Indians were cliff dwellers who lived in pueblos in northern New Mexico, northern Arizona, southern Utah, and southern Colorado until 1300 A.D. The beans in this chili, available at health food stores and by mail order (see Mail-Order Sources, page 217), were supposedly first cultivated by them. Note that the beans must soak overnight before you cook them.

Chili

- 1 pound dried Anasazi beans or pinto beans
- 2 tablespoons vegetable oil
- 2 pounds pork tenderloin or boneless pork, cut into ½-inch cubes
- Salt and freshly ground black pepper to taste
- 3 cups chopped white onion
- 3 red bell peppers, cored, seeded, and chopped into ¼-inch dice
- 4 cloves garlic, finely chopped
- 1 chipotle chile in adobo sauce, finely chopped
- 2 tablespoons adobo sauce
- 2 poblano chiles, roasted, peeled, seeded, and diced
- 2 tablespoons cumin seed, toasted and ground to a powder, or 1½ tablespoons ground cumin
- 1 tablespoon finely chopped oregano or 2 teaspoons dried
- 1 (12-ounce) bottle full-bodied beer
- 1 (28-ounce) can plum tomatoes, chopped, with juice reserved
- 8 lime wedges, for garnish
- ½ cup finely chopped cilantro leaves, for garnish
- ½ cup sour cream, for garnish
- 1 cup grated Monterey jack cheese, for garnish
- ½ cup finely chopped green onions, white and light green parts, for garnish
- Warmed tortillas, for accompaniment

In a large Dutch oven, cover the beans with water by 2 inches; allow to soak for 2 hours or overnight. Drain the beans, put them back in the pot, and cover with water again. Place the pot over medium heat, bring to a boil, reduce the heat, and simmer until the beans are tender, about 1 hour. Drain and reserve.

In the same Dutch oven, heat 1 tablespoon of the vegetable oil over medium heat. Season the pork cubes with salt and pepper and cook in batches, adding more oil as needed, and removing the meat as it is browned. In the same pan over medium heat, sauté the onion, peppers, and garlic until soft, about 10 minutes. Add the chipotle, adobo sauce, poblanos, cumin, oregano, and salt to taste. Reduce the heat and simmer for 10 minutes. Slowly stir in the beer and simmer 5 minutes more. Add the beans, tomatoes and their juice, and cooked pork. Simmer until the sauce has thickened somewhat and the pork is tender, about 1 hour.

Ladle the chili into bowls and pass the lime wedges, cilantro, sour cream, cheese, and green onions. Serve with warmed tortillas.

Vegetarian Red Bean Chili

Mary Sue Milliken and Susan Feniger

Serves 4 to 6

For their chunky, spicy stew, Mary Sue and Susan say, "Salvador red beans are the best we've found, but many types of beans would be great in this recipe—cranberry beans, kidney, or pinto."

2 cups dried red beans, washed and picked over

8 cups water

1 ancho chile, stemmed and seeded

⅓ cup olive oil

2 cups diced white onion

2 teaspoons salt

½ teaspoon freshly ground black pepper

5 cloves garlic, finely chopped

2 parsnips, peeled and cut into ½-inch chunks

2 carrots, peeled and cut into ½-inch chunks

2 stalks celery, peeled and cut into ½-inch chunks

1 zucchini, trimmed and cut into ½-inch chunks

1 yellow squash, trimmed and cut into ½-inch chunks

Ancho Chile Relish, for garnish (see page 209)

Place the beans and the water in a large saucepan or stockpot and bring to a boil over medium-high heat. Cover, reduce the heat, and simmer until the small beans are creamy, not powdery, 45 to 60 minutes. Remove from the heat.

Lightly toast the ancho chile over a low gas flame or a hot grill for a few seconds on each side, just until the skin bubbles. Set aside.

In a large skillet, heat the olive oil over medium heat. Sauté the onions, 1 teaspoon of the salt, and the pepper until the onions are golden, 8 to 10 minutes. Add the garlic, reduce the heat to low, and cook an additional minute to release the aromas.

Scrape the onions and garlic into the stockpot with the beans, along with the toasted ancho, parsnips, and carrots. Raise the heat to medium and bring the mixture to a boil; cover, reduce the heat, and simmer for 10 minutes. Add the celery, zucchini, yellow squash, and the remaining 1 teaspoon salt. Simmer, covered, until all the vegetables are soft, about 15 minutes longer. Remove any pieces of ancho chile.

Ladle into large bowls and serve hot with a dollop of ancho chile relish.

Be sure to cook the beans in a covered pot so they become creamy and the liquid doesn't boil away. Add salt to the chili after the beans have cooked, or their skins will get tough. To test for doneness: Take a very small bean from the pot. Put it on a work surface and press with your finger. A cooked bean is creamy through to its center; if it's still powdery, cook it longer.

Chicken Posole

The name for this ages-old New World stew is likely a variation of pozo, Spanish for "puddle." Posole and other corn-based dishes kept the native peoples of the Americas free of the disease pellagra, a niacin deficiency that plagued other cultures who were heavy corn consumers. To produce hominy, the Aztecs, Mayas, and Native Americans of the Southwest processed corn with an alkali, which not only removed its tough hull and made the kernel more digestible, but also released niacin for absorption by the body.

2 chicken breast halves, bone-in, skin removed

6 cups water

2 cups chopped white onion

5 long green chiles (Anaheim), roasted, peeled, seeded, and diced

2 teaspoons whole cumin seed, toasted and coarsely ground, or 1½ teaspoons ground cumin

1 teaspoon dried oregano

2 cups hominy (rinsed and drained if using canned)

Salt and freshly ground black pepper to taste

1 tablespoon freshly squeezed lime juice

Green Chile and Tomatillo Sauce (see page 195), for garnish

1 cup crumbled cotija cheese, Monterey jack, or queso fresco, for garnish

½ cup chopped green onions, white and light green parts, for garnish

Lime wedges, for garnish

Place chicken breasts in a large, heavy saucepan and cover with the water. Place the pan over medium heat and bring to a boil. Cover, reduce the heat, and simmer until the chicken breasts are cooked through, about 20 minutes. With tongs, remove the chicken from the pot, leaving the liquid behind. Allow chicken to cool. Add the chopped onion, green chiles, cumin, oregano, hominy, and salt and pepper to taste to the saucepan. Bring the mixture to a boil, reduce the heat, and simmer until the mixture is thickened slightly and the flavors are well blended, at least 1 hour. Remove the chicken from the bones, cut into ½-inch dice, and return to the pan. Cook until the chicken is warmed through, another 10 minutes. Add the lime juice, adjust the seasonings to taste, and serve in bowls garnished with green chile and tomatillo sauce, cheese, green onions, and lime wedges.

You can use leftover chicken or turkey instead of fresh chicken, but replace the water in the recipe with chicken stock. This stew freezes beautifully, so consider making a double batch.

Chapter 4

Main Courses

When the Spanish introduced cattle to the Southwest, beef, milk, and cheese became part of the regional diet. For cowboys on the range, though, even 200 years later, the beef they ate was anything but choice. Their meals were usually tough and tasteless scraps of meat made barely edible with simple seasoning and endless simmering. Occasionally, the results pleased even the dulled palate of the cowpoke. "Son-of-a-Bitch Stew," a slow-cooked "delicacy" chock-full of variety meats from a calf, was one that they took special pride in preparing.

Today's Southwestern chefs are just as prideful about the beef they cook, but of course much more selective of the cuts. Robert Del Grande buys his meats for Houston's Cafe Annie with the same connoisseurship he gives to restocking the wine list. His Coffee-Roasted Fillet of Beef with Pasilla Chile

Broth (see page 82) is as far from tough, tired trail food as you can get.

In Texas, beef also means barbecue. There, the word connotes long, slow smoking over indirect heat until the meat is meltingly tender and flavor-packed. And, naturally, it's not just a meal, but an event. It sometimes involves hundreds of guests and mind-boggling amounts of meat. At the helm are barbecue masters schooled in the fine points of pit cookery, and as respected by their minions as any four-star chef.

Brisket is the Texan's meat of choice, along with pork back ribs, chicken, and sausages. Traditionally, the meat was buried in a trench, smoked for hours over fragrant hardwood coals, and basted with explosive, vinegary sauces. Today the cooking is more often above ground on metal grates or bars, but the flavor is just as memorable. Chef Lenard Rubin's Southwestern Barbecue Paella (see page 103) is a minicourse in this Texas culinary art.

Just as famous as Texas 'cue is the legendary chuck wagon and its boss—called "cookie" or even "gut robber" by the trail hands. It was a title of respect, though, as they were dependent on his goodwill for their dinner. Chef Chuck Wiley is a modern-day cowboy cook who loves nothing more than to escape to the wide open spaces and grill up a great outdoor meal. But the creations of this Arizona "cookie," including Achiote-Basted Rack of Venison (see page 86) and Dutch Oven Green Chile Corn Bread (see page 154), is the stuff that trail hands only dreamed of.

But don't think the Southwest is all about just meat. Fish and game are plentiful in the region's many lakes, streams, and forests; even the desert teems with wildlife. Chef Robert McGrath grew up hunting and fishing in the Colorado mountains. His sophisticated cuisine, like Pan-Fried Canyon Trout (see page 113), is a celebration of this special bounty.

This chapter includes the main courses of today's Southwest in all their variety, from beef to fish to game to barbecue.

Ribeye Steaks with Red Chile Butter

Robert Del Grande   Serves 4

This is the perfect backyard entertaining entrée. The butter can be used for all sorts of other things: corn on the cob, to stuff under the skin of poultry, to float on steamed vegetables, or to spread on toasted bread.

Basting Sauce

4 tablespoons olive oil
2 tablespoons molasses
2 tablespoons red wine vinegar
1 teaspoon chile powder
½ teaspoon salt
½ teaspoon freshly ground black pepper

Red Chile Butter

1 ancho chile, stemmed and seeded
2 teaspoons olive oil
¼ cup coarsely chopped yellow onion
3 cloves garlic, coarsely chopped
½ cup unsalted butter, slightly softened
½ teaspoon freshly squeezed lime juice
¼ teaspoon maple syrup or brown sugar
⅛ teaspoon salt

2 well-marbled ribeye steaks, bone-in (24 to 32 ounces each)

Do Ahead { The marinade and the red chile butter can be made up to 2 days ahead, covered, and refrigerated. Extra chile butter is delicious on corn on the cob.

For the basting sauce: Combine all the ingredients in a small bowl; mix well. Set aside.

For the red chile butter: Soak the ancho chile in warm water to cover until soft, approximately 20 minutes. When soft, drain off the water. Heat the olive oil in a small skillet over medium-high heat. Add the onion and garlic and sauté until lightly caramelized, about 5 minutes. Remove from the heat and let cool to room temperature. On a cutting board, mince and mash the softened chile with a chef's knife until the consistency of a rough paste. Place the chile paste in a bowl. In the same manner, mince and mash the onion and garlic to a rough paste; add to the bowl. Add the butter, lime juice, syrup or sugar, and salt and mix well. Chill until ready to serve.

Prepare a hardwood charcoal fire. Keep the charcoal in a tight pile. When the fire is very hot, brush the steaks lightly with the basting sauce. Grill the steaks over the very hot charcoal until well seared, about 2 minutes per side. Brush the steaks with additional sauce as they cook. Spread the charcoals out very sparsely to reduce the heat of the charcoal fire and finish grilling the steaks slowly until medium-rare (internal temperature of 130°), another 10 to 15 minutes.

Remove the steaks from the grill and allow to stand for 10 to 15 minutes to let the juices settle. Carve the steaks into thin slices and serve immediately with the red chile butter.

Always buy the best-quality beef you can find, and from a trusted source.

Coffee~Roasted Fillet of Beef with Pasilla Chile Broth

Robert Del Grande

Serves 4 to 6

Chef Del Grande's unique method for roasting beef produces a succulent fillet that is perfectly cooked. The coffee and cocoa give the beef fragrance, which it doesn't naturally have, and an appealing color. The pasilla chile in the sauce has a slight coffee flavor that beautifully complements the meat.

Beef

2-pound fillet of beef (preferably cut from the large end of the whole fillet)

1 teaspoon salt

1 teaspoon freshly ground black pepper

2 tablespoons virgin olive oil

2 tablespoons very finely ground coffee beans

1 tablespoon unsweetened cocoa powder

⅛ teaspoon ground cinnamon

Pasilla Chile Broth

1 tablespoon unsalted butter

1 cup coarsely chopped white onion

6 whole cloves garlic, peeled

2 pasilla chiles (about ½ ounce), stemmed, seeded, and torn into large pieces

1 thick corn tortilla (about ¾ ounce), 6 inches in diameter, torn into pieces

2½ cups chicken stock, plus more if needed

¼ cup heavy cream

1 teaspoon salt

1 teaspoon brown sugar

Do Ahead { The pasilla broth can be made up to 2 days ahead. To store, cover tightly and refrigerate.

For the beef: Tie the fillet with butcher twine at ½-inch intervals. Rub the fillet well with the salt and pepper, then with the olive oil. In a small bowl, combine the ground coffee, cocoa powder, and cinnamon; mix well. Spread the mixture over a work surface and roll the fillet in the mixture to evenly coat the beef. Allow the beef to marinate approximately 30 minutes at room temperature.

For the pasilla chile broth: Heat a large saucepan over medium-high heat. Add the butter and sauté the onion and garlic until nicely browned, about 10 minutes. Add the pasilla chile and tortilla, reduce the heat slightly, and slowly sauté until golden brown, about another 10 minutes. Add the chicken stock, raise the heat and bring to a boil; reduce the heat and simmer, partially covered, for 10 minutes. Remove from the heat and let cool. Transfer the mixture to a blender and purée until smooth, about 1 minute. Strain back into the saucepan and add the cream, salt, and brown sugar. The sauce should not be too thick. If it is, thin with more chicken stock or water. Bring the pasilla broth to a boil over medium-high heat. Reduce the heat to low and simmer until ready to serve.

Preheat an oven to 400°. Place the fillet on a roasting rack in a roasting pan. Place in the middle of the oven and cook for 10 minutes. Immediately reduce the heat to 250°. After 20 minutes, check the internal temperature of the fillet (125° for medium-rare and 135° for medium). If further cooking is necessary, return the beef to the 250° oven and slowly roast to the desired temperature. Remove the fillet from the oven and keep warm. Let meat rest at least 10 minutes. Remove the string and carve. Continued page 84.

Shiitake Mushroom Garnish

2 tablespoons unsalted butter
¾ pound shiitake mushrooms, stems removed (and discarded), caps cut into quarters
Salt and freshly ground black pepper to taste
6 sprigs watercress
Gratin of Swiss Chard (see page 134), for accompaniment

For the shiitake mushroom garnish: Melt the 2 tablespoons butter over medium-high heat in a large skillet. Add the quartered shiitake mushrooms and sauté them quickly until browned, 3 to 5 minutes. Salt and pepper to taste and keep warm.

Assembly: Slice the beef fillet into ¼-inch slices and arrange in 4 to 6 large bowls or deep plates. Ladle some of the pasilla broth over the slices of beef. Spoon some of the sautéed mushrooms over the beef and garnish with watercress sprigs. Serve with gratin of swiss chard, if desired.

Barbecued Beef Short Ribs

Lenard Rubin

Serves 4

Barbecue is meat slow-cooked for hours over relatively low heat. The result is tender, succulent, and falls off the bone. The Mango-Chipotle Barbecue Sauce updates this terrific example of classic Texas barbecue.

These ribs are part of Lenard's grand Southwestern Barbecue Paella (see page 103), but work beautifully on their own.

1 tablespoon salt
1 tablespoon freshly ground black pepper
1 tablespoon paprika
1 tablespoon brown sugar
2 teaspoons dry mustard
1 teaspoon cayenne pepper
4 beef short ribs
½ cup hickory, apple, cherry, or other wood chips, soaked in warm water for at least 20 minutes
2 cups Mango-Chipotle Barbecue Sauce (see page 193)

Mix all the dry ingredients together and rub on all sides of the short ribs. Cover and refrigerate overnight.

Remove the ribs from the refrigerator and bring to room temperature. Preheat a charcoal barbecue grill with cover or a smoker. When the grill or smoker temperature is about 225°, add about 1 tablespoon of the wood chips to the coals. Maintain the same temperature throughout the cooking process by adjusting the cover or vents and adding more charcoal, if needed.

Place the ribs on the grill and cook for 2 hours, adding more soaked wood chips every 30 minutes. Cook for another 2 hours, gradually using less and less chips so the smoke is eventually gone. Place the ribs in one layer on a small baking pan and spoon 1 cup barbecue sauce over the ribs. Cover the pan with foil. Continue cooking in the 225° grill or smoker for another hour, basting with about ¼ cup barbecue sauce every 20 minutes. The meat should be tender, juicy, and falling off the bone. Remove from the baking pan and put the ribs directly on the hot grill to crisp them. Brush on remaining sauce and serve immediately.

Nopales Stuffed with Beef Machaca

Jay McCarthy   Serves 8

Machaca, a Mexican dish of shredded meat seasoned with chiles and onions, is often stuffed into tortillas for tacos, burritos, or flautas. Here the container is nopales, the pads of the prickly pear cactus. According to Jay, the Aztecs would stuff nopales with game, sew them up with threads from the agave plant (the source of tequila), and slowly roast them on hot stones.

Machaca

- 5 pounds boneless beef chuck roast, trimmed of fat
- 1 tablespoon olive oil
- 2 cups finely chopped white onions
- 5 jalapeño chiles, seeded and finely chopped
- 2 teaspoons finely chopped garlic
- 1 tablespoon ground cumin
- 3 tablespoons chile powder
- 1 cinnamon stick
- 1 cup chopped tomatoes, including juice
- 2 teaspoons dried oregano
- 3 bay leaves
- 8 cups beef stock, plus more if needed
- Salt and freshly ground black pepper to taste
- ½ cup chopped cilantro

- 8 cactus pads (nopales)

Do Ahead { Machaca is actually better the day after it is cooked, so it could be made 1 or 2 days ahead. The pads should be prepared shortly before baking or they will dry out.

For the machaca: Heat a large, heavy pot or Dutch oven over medium-high heat. Add the chuck roast and brown well on all sides, remove the meat from the pan and set aside. Add the olive oil to the pot; when hot, add the onions, jalapeños, and garlic. Sauté until softened, about 5 minutes. Add the cumin, chile powder, cinnamon stick, tomatoes, oregano, bay leaves, stock, salt, and pepper. Bring to a boil.

Preheat an oven to 350°. Put the beef back into the pot with the stock mixture; cover and cook until the beef shreds easily with a fork, 4 to 5 hours. Check occasionally; add more stock or water if necessary. Let the beef cool in any remaining liquid. Remove the bay leaves and cinnamon stick.

For the cactus pads: With a sharp paring knife, remove the thorns and "eyes" from each pad; trim around the edges of the pad. Carefully make a slit along the length of each pad to form a pocket (like pita bread).

When the beef is cool enough to handle, use a fork to shred it into bite-sized strings; stir them into any accumulated juices in the bottom of the baking pan. If there is too much liquid, place the pot over medium heat and cook until the liquid is reduced. Stir in the cilantro. Fill the cactus pockets with the beef mixture and place on a baking sheet. Bake until the cactus pads are tender and the beef is warmed through, about 30 minutes. Serve 1 stuffed pad per person. Use any leftover machaca for quesadillas, burritos, or flautas.

The pads keep the filling very moist. If made with small pads, this dish is a great appetizer. When making the machaca, the meat is done when it shreds with a fork.

Achiote~Basted Rack of Venison

Chuck Wiley

Serves 4

Chuck prefers to make his own Achiote Paste (see page 205); if you are using packaged, mix it with enough orange juice to make a thick sauce. For nonhunters, you can order fresh venison by mail (see Mail-Order Sources, page 217). This same recipe also works very well with loin of pork, pork chops, or pork tenderloin; adjust the cooking time accordingly.

To complete the menu, serve Chuck's Roasted Vegetables (see page 144) and Dutch Oven Green Chile Corn Bread (see page 154).

1 rack of venison (about 1½ pounds)
Salt and freshly ground black pepper to taste
1 cup Achiote Paste (see page 205)

Preheat an oven to 400°. Season the venison with salt and pepper to taste. Heat a large skillet over high heat; when very hot, add the venison and sear each side until golden brown. Remove from the skillet and brush the venison liberally with achiote paste. Place on a rack in a roasting pan and roast until rare to medium-rare (125° to 130° internal temperature), brushing with more of the paste, 20 to 30 minutes. Remove from the oven, cover loosely with aluminum foil, and keep warm until ready to serve. Cut into chops and serve immediately.

Before the venison is roasted in the oven, it is first seared, which caramelizes the surface for more flavor and so the meat accepts more of the baste.

Cumin~Cured Pork Tenderloin with Avocado Salsa

The spice rub adds just the right amount of flavor to the pork and gives it a light crust. The creamy, chunky avocado salsa is the perfect foil to the spicy rub and adds another layer of texture. It's important not to overcook the pork, so it stays moist. Use a meat thermometer and allow the meat to rest before slicing.

Rub

- 2 tablespoons cumin seed, toasted
- 2 tablespoons black peppercorns
- 1 tablespoon salt
- 1 shallot, chopped
- 1 clove garlic, chopped
- 1 tablespoon olive oil, plus more if needed

- 2 pounds pork tenderloin, trimmed
- 2 tablespoons olive oil

Salsa

- 1 large Haas avocado, peeled and diced
- 2 tablespoons freshly squeezed lime juice
- Zest of 1 lime, finely chopped
- 1 tablespoon chopped cilantro
- 1 tablespoon gold tequila
- ¼ cup chopped green onions, white and green parts
- 1 jalapeño chile, stemmed, seeded, and finely chopped
- ½ cup diced red or yellow bell pepper
- Salt and freshly ground black pepper to taste

Do Ahead { The spice rub can be made a day ahead, covered, and refrigerated. The salsa can be made up to 4 hours ahead, covered and, refrigerated.

For the rub: With a mortar and pestle or in the bowl of a mini food processor, pulse together the cumin seed and peppercorns. Add the salt, shallot, garlic, and olive oil and mix until a thick paste forms, adding more olive oil, if necessary. Rub the paste over the pork tenderloins and refrigerate, covered, for at least 2 hours or overnight.

To cook the pork: Preheat an oven to 350°. Remove the meat from the refrigerator and bring to room temperature. Rub off the excess spice mixture. In a large, heavy skillet, heat the 2 tablespoons olive oil over medium-high heat; when smoking, add the meat and sear on all sides. Transfer to a baking pan and finish cooking in the oven until the pork reaches an internal temperature of 150°, 15 to 20 minutes. Alternatively, the pork can be grilled on a preheated hot barbecue for approximately the same amount of time.

For the salsa: In a nonreactive bowl, combine all the ingredients.

Assembly: Allow the meat to rest for 5 to 10 minutes. Slice diagonally into ½-inch-thick slices. Arrange 4 to 5 slices on each of 6 plates and spoon about ⅓ cup salsa alongside the pork. Serve immediately.

Spice~Rubbed Pork Tenderloin in Corn Husks

Serves 6

Corn husks are a terrific wrapper for tamales, but also for many other fillings. They keep the filling moist, impart a wonderful corn flavor, and make a lovely presentation. This is the perfect entertaining dish. It requires just 20 minutes in the oven and can cook while your guests finish their soup.

Southwest Spice Rub

2 teaspoons cumin seed

2 teaspoons whole coriander seed

2 tablespoons chile powder

2 teaspoons sugar

1 teaspoon salt

1 teaspoon black peppercorns

½ teaspoon cayenne pepper

1½ pounds pork tenderloin, trimmed and cut into 6 equal pieces

9 dried corn husks, soaked in warm water until soft, about 1 hour, cleaned, and patted dry

Dried Cherry Salsa (see page 202), for accompaniment

Do Ahead { The spice mix can be made months ahead, and the pork packages themselves can be assembled a day ahead if covered with a damp towel (so the corn husks don't dry out) and refrigerated. The dried cherry salsa can be made a day ahead without the cilantro; add the cilantro just before serving.

For the spice rub: Place the cumin seed in a small dry skillet over medium-high heat and toast until lightly browned and aromatic. Transfer into a mini food processor, coffee grinder, or spice grinder and purée. Toast the coriander in the same skillet and add to the cumin in the grinder. Purée again. Add the remaining ingredients and purée until well blended. Turn out onto a plate.

Preheat an oven to 375°.

Roll each piece of pork in the spice mix and place in the center of a corn husk. Tear 3 corn husks into strips. Wrap the corn husk around the pork and tie each end with a corn husk strip. Repeat with the remaining pieces of pork and corn husks. Place the pork packages on a baking sheet and bake until a meat thermometer registers 145°, 25 to 30 minutes.

To serve, place one package on each plate and remove the corn husk strip from one end. Fold the corn husk back to expose the meat. Serve with dried cherry salsa.

Make more of the rub than you need for this recipe, and keep the extra stored airtight in the pantry. It's also a great gift, especially for someone who doesn't live in the Southwest, but craves the flavors.

Chicken and Tomatillo Tamales

John Rivera Sedlar　　　　　**Makes about 8**

John makes many types of exotic tamales, but these are the most traditional and very delicious. The most efficient way to assemble them (or any tamale) is assembly-line fashion: Lay the husks out on the counter, then work down the row to fill and tie them. These tamales freeze beautifully, so you might want to make more than one batch.

Tamale Dough

1 pound fresh masa or 1½ cups masa harina mixed with ¾ cup water

3 tablespoons vegetable shortening

1 teaspoon salt

½ teaspoon baking powder

⅛ teaspoon ground white pepper

⅓ to ½ cup chicken stock, at room temperature

Filling

1 cup Green Chile and Tomatillo Sauce (see page 195)

1 cup shredded cooked chicken

8 to 10 dried corn husks, soaked in warm water until soft, about 1 hour, cleaned, and patted dry

Do Ahead } The green chile and tomatillo sauce can be made up to 3 days ahead of assembly, covered, and refrigerated. The tamales can be made ahead and frozen, uncooked. Increase steaming time to 1 hour if frozen.

For the tamale dough: Bring the masa and the vegetable shortening to room temperature. Place the masa, shortening, salt, baking powder, and pepper in the bowl of an electric mixer fitted with the paddle attachment. Mix the ingredients for 10 minutes on low to medium speed, occasionally cleaning the sides of the bowl with a rubber spatula. Continue mixing while slowly drizzling the chicken stock into the bowl for another 5 minutes. The masa should not be too wet to the touch.

For the filling: In a bowl, mix the sauce and the chicken.

Assembly: With the bowl side of a large spoon, rub a thin layer of tamale dough across the center of a husk. Place 3 to 4 tablespoons of the filling into the center of the dough. Pull the sides of the husk up and around the fillings and fold over the pointed end. Pinch closed the wide end of the tamales. Continue making tamales until all the filling is used up.

Bring water to a boil over high heat in a steamer. Place the tamales on a perforated pan above the boiling water, reduce the heat, and steam the tamales until the masa is firm, about 45 minutes. Serve immediately.

 The hallmark of a good tamale is one that is very thin, very elegant, and very light. It's best to mix the masa for as much as 15 to 20 minutes so it's very light—the consistency of smooth cake frosting.

Chicken Breasts with Achiote Butter

Serves 4

The achiote butter adds flavor to the chicken, keeps it moist, and gives it beautiful color. Try this also with your next turkey.

Achiote Butter

4 tablespoons unsalted butter, softened

1 tablespoon Achiote Paste (see page 205)

4 chicken breast halves, bone-in, with skin

Salt and freshly ground black pepper to taste

4 wedges lime

For the achiote butter: In a small bowl, combine the butter and achiote paste until smooth and well combined.

Prepare a barbecue grill to high heat.

Loosen the skin of the chicken breasts so a pocket is formed between the skin and the flesh. With a spoon or your hands, stuff 1 tablespoon of Achiote Butter in the pocket, spreading to cover the surface of the chicken breast. Season the chicken breasts with salt and pepper to taste.

If using a gas grill, lower the barbecue to medium heat; if grilling over coals, let them cool to medium heat. Place the stuffed chicken breasts, skin side down, on the preheated grill. Cook 2 to 3 minutes and turn over. Cook until the flesh is no longer pink and the juices run clear, another 7 to 10 minutes. Remove from the grill. Garnish each serving with a wedge of lime and serve immediately.

Chicken with Red Pepper–Corn Sauce

Serves 8

For this lively vegetable sauce, it's worth your while to buy fresh-picked corn from a local farmers' market. Not only do you use the kernels, but you scrape the "milk" from the cob into the sauce, and you want both to be extra sweet. Marinating the chicken takes the most time. The rest goes together very quickly.

Marinade

½ cup vegetable oil
2 chipotle chiles in adobo sauce, finely chopped
½ cup freshly squeezed orange juice
2 tablespoons chopped cilantro
1 tablespoon chopped garlic

8 boneless, skinless chicken breast halves

Red Pepper–Corn Sauce

1 ear corn, husked
1 clove garlic, chopped
2 shallots, peeled and chopped
1 red jalapeño chile, diced
1 cup chicken stock
2 red bell peppers, roasted, peeled, seeded, and diced
Salt and freshly ground black pepper to taste

2 tablespoons corn oil

For the marinade: Combine all marinade ingredients together in a shallow glass dish. Place the chicken breasts in the dish with the marinade and turn to coat all sides. Cover with plastic wrap and refrigerate for at least 2 hours or overnight.

For the red pepper–corn sauce: Cut the corn kernels from the cob and set the cob aside. Place the corn kernels, garlic, shallots, jalapeño, and chicken stock in a saucepan over high heat and bring to a boil. Reduce the heat and simmer for 15 minutes. Scrape the corn cob with the back of a knife over the mixture to extract the corn germ; stir into the chicken stock mixture. Transfer to a blender, add the roasted bell peppers, and purée until smooth. Season with salt and pepper to taste and keep warm.

Remove the chicken breasts from the marinade and pat dry. Season with salt and pepper to taste. In a large, heavy skillet, heat the corn oil over medium heat. Sauté the breasts until lightly browned on the bottom, about 3 minutes; turn over and cook until golden brown on the other side and the juices run clear, about 3 minutes more. Keep warm.

Place a few tablespoons of sauce on each of 8 serving plates. Cut each piece of chicken into slices diagonally and arrange on top of the sauce. Serve immediately.

You can buy good-quality canned or boxed stock now, so making your own for this sauce isn't that important. Be sure, though, that the stock you buy isn't overly salted.

Marinated Chicken

Lenard Rubin   **Serves** 4

A complex sauce gives this chicken a special depth of flavor. Lenard includes it in his Southwestern Barbecue Paella (see page 103), but it's delicious on its own—a great choice for summer grilling.

Ancho Chile Purée

1 cup boiling water
1 ancho chile
1 teaspoon olive oil
¼ teaspoon chopped garlic
½ teaspoon chopped onion
1 tablespoon apple juice

2 tablespoons finely chopped garlic
3 tablespoons balsamic vinegar
3 tablespoons frozen orange juice concentrate, thawed
2 tablespoons grated orange zest
¼ cup honey
¼ cup olive oil
3 tablespoons freshly squeezed lime juice
3 tablespoons chopped cilantro
3 tablespoons soy sauce
2 tablespoons freshly ground black pepper
2 tablespoons ground cumin

4 chicken thighs, bone-in, with skin

Do Ahead { The marinade can be made up to 2 days ahead of time, covered, and refrigerated.

For the ancho chile purée: Pour the boiling water over the chile in a small bowl; let sit 20 minutes. Discard the water; remove the stem and seeds from the chile and coarsely chop into pieces. Heat the oil in a small saucepan over medium heat. Add the garlic, onion, and ancho chile. Cook until the onion and garlic are lightly browned, about 2 minutes. Add the apple juice and cook until almost all the liquid has evaporated. Pour the mixture into a blender and purée until smooth.

Pour the ancho purée into a bowl. Add the remaining ingredients except for the chicken; whisk together. Add the chicken and marinate; refrigerate for at least 4 hours or overnight.

Preheat a barbecue grill. When hot, place the chicken thighs on the grill; cook until the chicken begins to brown, about 3 minutes. Turn over and cook another 3 minutes. Move to a cooler portion of the grill and, if possible, cover for the remainder of the cooking process. Cook until the juices run clear when pierced with a toothpick or the point of a knife, about another 15 minutes, basting and turning constantly to avoid burning. Serve immediately.

Ancho~Glazed Chicken

Mary Sue Milliken and Susan Feniger   **Serves 6**

The chefs use one of their favorite chiles—the aromatic, coffee-scented ancho—in a marinade that is basically an ancho chile sauce. Use it in any recipe that calls for a red sauce.

Marinade

7 ancho chiles, stemmed and seeded

½ cup white vinegar

2 cups water, plus 1 or 2 tablespoons if needed

2 tablespoons olive oil

1 cup diced onion

4 cloves garlic, minced

2 teaspoons ground cumin

1 teaspoon dried oregano

2½ teaspoons salt

1 teaspoon freshly ground black pepper

Paste

2 tablespoons brown sugar

¼ cup freshly squeezed orange juice

3 tablespoons freshly squeezed lemon juice

2 tablespoons tomato paste

6 chicken breast halves, bone-in, skin removed

Salt and freshly ground black pepper to taste

Chipotle-Corn Relish (see page 210), for accompaniment (optional)

Seared Chard (see page 132), for accompaniment (optional)

Do Ahead { The marinade and the paste can be made 2 to 3 days ahead and kept, tightly covered, in the refrigerator.

For the marinade: In a heavy skillet over medium-high heat, toast the chiles until soft and brown, turning frequently to avoid scorching, 2 to 3 minutes. Transfer the toasted chiles to a saucepan and add the vinegar and 1 cup of the water. Bring to a boil, reduce the heat and simmer 10 minutes to soften the chiles. Transfer the chiles and liquid to a blender and purée until a smooth paste is formed, adding 1 or 2 tablespoons of water, if necessary. Set aside.

Heat the olive oil in a saucepan over medium-high heat; add the onions and sauté until deep golden brown, 8 to 10 minutes. Stir in the garlic, cumin, oregano, salt, and pepper; cook another minute. Add the reserved chile paste and sauté 2 to 3 minutes, stirring frequently. Add the remaining cup of water, bring to a boil, reduce the heat, and simmer 10 minutes. Remove half of the sauce from the pan and put into a bowl to cool (this will be the marinade).

For the paste: In a small bowl, mix together the brown sugar, orange and lemon juices, and tomato paste. Add to the remaining sauce in the pan and cook the mixture for another 15 minutes. Remove from the heat and set aside.

Season the chicken breasts with salt and pepper to taste. Coat the breasts generously with the cooled ancho marinade and put in a glass dish or heavy plastic bag; refrigerate and allow to marinate 2 to 4 hours or overnight.

Remove the breasts from the refrigerator. Preheat a broiler. Place the breasts directly on a baking sheet under the broiler; sear about 1 minute on each side. Brush with the ancho paste. Preheat an oven to 350°. Bake until the juices run clear, another 15 to 20 minutes, turning frequently and brushing with additional ancho paste. Remove from the oven. Place a chicken breast on each of 6 plates. Serve immediately with chipotle-corn relish and seared chard, if desired.

Contemporary Chicken Mole

Donna Nordin   Serves 8

A classic mole starts with 26 different ingredients, as Donna points out. But most cooks don't want to work with that many. She's modernized this traditional dish to make it more "kitchen friendly" with fewer ingredients, but just as good a flavor.

Mole

3 dried red New Mexico chiles, stemmed and seeded

3 ancho chiles, stemmed and seeded

4 dried pasilla chiles (substitute chile negro), stemmed and seeded

4 tablespoons olive oil

1 white onion, stemmed and cut into quarters

5 cloves of garlic, peeled

1 banana, peeled and cut into 1-inch pieces

¼ cup dried cranberries

¼ cup peanuts

¼ cup almonds

4 tomatillos, husked, washed, and roasted (see page 216)

1 tomato, roasted and cored (see page 216)

3 cups chicken stock

1 croissant, toasted

2 flour tortillas, 8 inches in diameter, well toasted so they're lightly charred

1 poblano chile, roasted, peeled, and seeded

2 jalapeño chiles, roasted, peeled, and seeded

1 tablet (3.1 ounces) Ibarra Mexican chocolate, coarsely chopped

1 tablespoon brown sugar

1 tablespoon freshly ground espresso or coffee

For the mole: Place a large, heavy-bottomed skillet over medium-high heat. When hot, add the dried New Mexico, ancho, and pasilla chiles and toast until slightly softened and fragrant, about 1 minute per side. Remove from the skillet and place in a large bowl of warm water; let stand until the chiles soften, about 30 minutes.

In the same skillet, heat 2 tablespoons of the olive oil over medium heat; when hot, add the quartered onion and garlic. Sauté until lightly browned, about 5 minutes. Add the banana, cranberries, peanuts, and almonds to the skillet; continue cooking 5 minutes more. Transfer the mixture in the skillet to a blender. Add the roasted tomatillos, tomato, and ½ cup of the stock; purée. Add the croissant and tortillas and additional stock as needed, about 1½ cups more; purée. Add the poblano and jalapeños and blend until smooth. Pour the blended ingredients into a large saucepan over medium-high heat. Bring to a boil, reduce the heat to low and simmer for 30 minutes. The mixture will sputter and spatter.

Remove the soaked chiles from the water with a slotted spoon and place into the blender. Add about ⅓ cup of the soaking water, purée, and add to the mixture in the saucepan. Also add any remaining stock to the saucepan and cook, still at a simmer, for 30 minutes more.

Add the chocolate, sugar, and ground coffee to the mole. Simmer another 10 minutes and add salt and pepper to taste.

Preheat an oven to 375°. In a heavy skillet, add the remaining 2 tablespoons olive oil and heat over medium-high heat. Season the chicken breasts with salt and pepper to taste and add to the hot oil. Sear until browned, about 2 minutes per side. Transfer the chicken to a casserole dish large enough to hold the breasts in one layer. Spoon enough mole over the breasts to coat them generously; save the remaining mole for another use. Bake the casserole until the chicken is cooked through, 15 to 20 minutes.

Place 2 chicken breast halves on each plate. Sprinkle with toasted sesame seed and garnish with a sprig of cilantro.

Salt and freshly ground black
   pepper to taste

16 boneless, skinless chicken
   breast halves
2 tablespoons sesame seed,
   toasted, for garnish
8 sprigs cilantro, for garnish

Mexican chocolate contains ground almonds, cinnamon, and sugar, and comes in tablet form. If you can't find it, per ounce of Mexican chocolate, substitute 1 ounce semisweet chocolate, ½ teaspoon ground cinnamon, and 1 drop almond extract.

Green Chile~Sour Cream Chicken Breasts

Serves 4

If you fear the chile's awesome fire power, rest assured that the sour cream will douse some of the heat. Dairy products are proven chile tamers.

1 tablespoon olive oil
4 boneless, skinless chicken
   breast halves
Salt and freshly ground black
   pepper to taste
½ cup chopped green onions,
   white and light green parts
1 tablespoon finely chopped
   garlic
1 cup chicken stock
2 poblano chiles, roasted,
   peeled, seeded, and diced
2 tablespoons finely chopped
   cilantro
1 teaspoon cumin seed, toasted
   and ground, or ¾ teaspoon
   ground cumin
½ cup sour cream

Heat the olive oil in a large skillet over medium heat. Season the chicken breasts with salt and pepper to taste and add to the hot oil. Cook until just firm to the touch, 2 to 3 minutes per side. Remove from the heat and keep warm.

Add the green onions and garlic to the skillet, and cook 2 to 3 minutes, stirring constantly so the garlic doesn't burn. Add the chicken stock and cook another 5 minutes. Add the chiles, cilantro, and cumin, and cook until the liquid is reduced to about ½ cup. Reduce the heat to low and whisk in the sour cream. Add the chicken and any juices back to the skillet and cook until the chicken is warmed through and the sauce is hot, about 5 minutes, turning the chicken to coat. Serve immediately.

Sugar~ and Chile~Cured Duck Breasts

Robert McGrath

Serves 4

This is Robert's contemporary take on trail food, inspired by the Old West. It's a whole other world from hardtack, however, and lots more fun to eat.

¼ cup granulated sugar

3 tablespoons ancho chile powder

1 tablespoon salt

4 boneless, skinless duck breasts (8 ounces each)

Sauce

1 tablespoon unsalted butter

1 cup corn kernels

1 teaspoon chopped shallot

1 cup white wine

4 tablespoons cold unsalted butter, cut into 4 pieces

3 tablespoons Red Bell Pepper Ketchup (see page 196) or regular ketchup

Green Chile Macaroni (see page 143), for accompaniment

1 tablespoon snipped chives, for garnish

In a small bowl, mix together the sugar, chile powder, and salt. Evenly rub the mixture over the duck breasts; place on a plate and refrigerate for at least 2 hours.

For the sauce: In a saucepan, heat the butter over medium heat. Add the corn and cook until softened, about 2 minutes. Add the shallot and white wine. Bring to a boil, reduce the heat, and simmer until the liquid is reduced by half, about 10 minutes. Let cool slightly and put in a blender; purée until smooth. Add the cold butter, one piece at a time, until incorporated. Strain the sauce back into the saucepan and keep warm. Just before serving, stir in the ketchup.

Assembly: Prepare a barbecue grill. When hot, brush off the excess dry cure from the duck breasts and place the breasts on the grill. Cook until still pink inside, 5 to 7 minutes per side.

Spoon about ½ cup green chile macaroni off-center onto each of 4 plates. Cut the duck breasts diagonally into thin slices and rest the slices up against the mound of macaroni. Spoon the corn sauce over the open portion of the plate and top with chopped chives.

 For best flavor, let the duck breasts sit in the chile cure overnight before cooking. Cracklings made with leftover duck skin are a real treat and a great garnish: Put the skin in a very hot oven to render all the fat and to get crispy. Then cut it up and sprinkle on the duck breasts just before serving.

Duck Breasts with Raspberry~ Chipotle Sauce

Serves 8

This sauce is also delicious on pork. It's not necessary to use fresh raspberries; individually frozen ones (but not sweetened) work just as well. If using frozen, allow them to thaw and include any accumulated juices.

2 tablespoons rendered duck fat
  or vegetable oil
4 boneless, skinless duck
  breasts (about 12 ounces
  each)
Salt and freshly ground black
  pepper to taste

Sauce

2 tablespoons finely chopped
  shallots
2 cloves garlic, finely chopped
1½ cups raspberries
1 cup dry red wine
2 cups chicken or duck stock,
  preferably homemade
1 canned chipotle chile in adobo
  sauce, puréed
2 tablespoons unsalted butter,
  at room temperature
Salt and freshly ground black
  pepper to taste

Heat the duck fat in a heavy skillet over medium heat until it is hot, but not smoking. Pat the duck breasts dry, season with salt and pepper to taste, and cook in the hot fat, turning once, for 6 to 8 minutes, or until they are springy to the touch. Remove the breasts from the skillet and keep warm.

For the sauce: Pour off all but 1 tablespoon of fat remaining in the skillet. Sauté the shallots and garlic in the fat for about 30 seconds. Add the raspberries and cook, stirring, another 30 seconds. Add the red wine, scraping up any bits on the bottom of the pan (this is called deglazing). Reduce the mixture over high heat until about ¾ cup liquid remains. Add the stock and chipotle purée. Reduce over high heat until about 2 cups liquid remain. Strain the mixture into a clean saucepan and heat to boiling. Whisk in the butter and season with salt and pepper to taste.

Cut the duck breasts diagonally into thin slices. Spoon some of the sauce onto 8 heated plates and arrange the duck slices over it.

Tequila Sunrise Fettucine

Serves 4

Giving its name to this chicken-and-pasta dish is a colorful cocktail that reminds romantics of the flames of color that light up the Southwestern morning sky. The chicken briefly marinates in adobo sauce, which comes canned with chipotle chiles. If it's not on hand, substitute any chile sauce, or, for a less spicy dish, don't use it at all.

½ cup chicken stock
2 tablespoons tequila
2 tablespoons freshly squeezed orange juice
1 tablespoon grenadine syrup
¼ cup Mexican Cream (see page 203) or sour cream
2 cups diced raw chicken
1 tablespoon adobo sauce (from a can of chipotle chiles)
2 tablespoons unsalted butter
½ cup chopped red onion
1 tablespoon finely chopped jalapeño chile
1 cup diced red bell pepper (about 1 pepper)
1 cup diced yellow bell pepper (about 1 pepper)
2 teaspoons finely chopped garlic
¼ cup finely chopped cilantro
Salt and freshly ground black pepper to taste
2 teaspoons salt (for pasta cooking water)
12 ounces fettucine
2 tablespoons chopped cilantro, for garnish (optional)

Do Ahead The chicken-chile and Mexican cream mixtures can be made up to 4 hours ahead and refrigerated. Bring both mixtures to room temperature before adding them to the sautéed vegetables.

In a small saucepan, combine the chicken stock, tequila, orange juice, and grenadine. Over medium heat reduce the mixture to ⅓ cup. Let cool. Stir in the Mexican cream and set aside.

In a nonreactive bowl, toss the diced raw chicken with adobo sauce. Set aside.

In a large skillet, melt the butter over medium heat. Add the onion, jalapeño, and bell peppers, and cook, stirring occasionally, until the vegetables are soft, about 5 minutes. Add the garlic and cilantro and cook 1 minute more. Add the chicken-chile mixture and the stock-cream mixture to the skillet and bring to a boil. Reduce the heat and simmer gently until the chicken is cooked and the sauce is thick, 3 to 5 minutes. Season with salt and pepper to taste.

Bring a large pot of water to a rolling boil. Add the 2 teaspoons salt and fettucine. Cook until al dente, 8 to 10 minutes. Drain well but do not rinse.

Toss the sauce with the well-drained fettucine and divide among 4 plates. Garnish with additional chopped cilantro, if desired.

Southwestern Barbecue Paella

Lenard Rubin   Serves 4

This labor of love will be well worth it when you sit down to the table. If it looks too daunting, make the rice base and add whatever seafood, poultry, or meat components you like. Or invite friends over and make it a group effort. Many of the elements can be prepared ahead, so make a timetable and start grilling.

Corn

1 ear corn in the husk
2 tablespoons unsalted butter
1 teaspoon chile powder
½ teaspoon ground cumin
Salt and freshly ground black
  pepper to taste

Mushrooms

2 portobello mushrooms
2 tablespoons olive oil
Salt and freshly ground black
  pepper to taste
2 tablespoons balsamic vinegar

1 chorizo sausage link

Cactus pads

4 prickly pear cactus pads
  (nopales) or 4 (3 x ½-inch)
  slices zucchini
1 tablespoon olive oil
Salt and freshly ground black
  pepper to taste

Do Ahead { The link chorizo, mushrooms, peppers, and chiles can be prepared a day ahead and refrigerated. The marinade for the chicken and the sauce for the ribs can be made up to 2 days ahead, covered, and refrigerated.

Prepare a barbecue grill.

For the corn: Pull back the layers of husk on the corn and remove the silk. In a small bowl, combine the melted butter, chili powder, cumin, salt, and pepper. Rub the corn kernels with the butter mixture and fold the husk back around the corn. Tie at the top with kitchen string. Soak the corn in cold water for about 8 minutes so that it doesn't burn when grilled. Remove from the water, pat dry, and cook over hot coals, turning often, until done, about 20 minutes. Remove from the heat. Shuck and cut in half lengthwise; then cut in half crosswise into quarters.

For the mushrooms: Cut the stems off the mushrooms and remove the gills on the underside by gently scraping with the edge of a small knife. Rub the mushrooms with 1 tablespoon of the olive oil and place, top side down, on the hot grill. Cook for a few minutes and turn over; cook for 2 minutes more and turn over again. Season with salt and pepper to taste and cook until the mushrooms soften and they begin to seep liquid, about 5 minutes. Remove from the heat and sprinkle with balsamic vinegar and the remaining tablespoon olive oil. Let cool and cut into fourths.

Rice base

½ cup olive oil

½ cup finely chopped onions

¼ cup finely chopped garlic

1 cup diced tomatoes

1 cup bulk chorizo sausage

1 teaspoon saffron threads

4 jumbo shrimp (15 per pound),
    peeled and deveined

1½ cups Texmati rice

2½ cups chicken stock, heated
    to a simmer

1 cup cooked black beans

1 cup green peas

¼ cup chopped cilantro

Salt and freshly ground black
    pepper to taste

4 Green Lip mussels

4 littleneck clams

4 Marinated Chicken thighs (see
    page 93)

Barbecued Beef Short Ribs (see
    page 84)

2 red bell peppers, roasted,
    seeded, peeled, and diced

2 poblano chiles, roasted,
    seeded, peeled, and diced

¼ cup finely chopped cilantro

For the chorizo sausage link: Bring a medium pot of water to a boil over high heat. Add the sausage link, reduce the heat, and simmer until the sausage is firm, about 15 minutes. Grill the sausage until crispy, turning frequently so it cooks evenly without burning, about 10 minutes. Cool and slice into 4 diagonal pieces.

For the cactus pads: Trim around the outside edge of the cactus pads with a small knife, then gently slide the knife flat across each side of the pads to remove spines. Rub the cleaned pads (or zucchini) with the olive oil and cook on the hot grill for 3 minutes on each side (they should be softened but still slightly crunchy). Season with salt and pepper to taste.

For the rice base: Heat the olive oil in a paella pan, *casuela*, or large skillet over medium-high heat. Add the onions and garlic and cook until lightly browned, about 10 minutes. Add the tomatoes and cook, stirring, until they dissolve into the onions and garlic, about 10 minutes more. Add the bulk chorizo and cook 2 minutes; add the saffron and stir well. Scrape ingredients aside to make room on the bottom of the pan for the shrimp; cook the shrimp 1 minute, turn over and cook for another minute. Stir the shrimp into the other ingredients in the pan and cook an additional minute. Remove the shrimp and set aside (they should be about three-fourths cooked). Add the rice and stir for about 2 minutes. Add 1 cup of the hot stock and bring to a boil; reduce the heat and simmer. Stir the rice every 5 minutes, adding more stock a little at a time as it is absorbed, until the rice is thoroughly cooked, about 20 minutes from the time it begins to simmer. Add the black beans, peas, and cilantro. Stir well and season with salt and pepper to taste. Arrange the reserved shrimp, corn, portobellos, cactus pads (or zucchini), chorizo slices, mussels, and clams as desired over the top of the rice, leaving enough room for the chicken and ribs. Cover the pan and cook over medium heat until the clams and mussels open up and all ingredients are hot, 8 to 10 minutes. Remove the hot chicken and ribs from the barbecue grill and add to the paella. Scatter the red bell peppers, poblano chiles, and cilantro over all. Bring the paella pan to the table and divide among 4 large plates.

Green Chile Fettucine with Shrimp

Serves 6

The green pasta contrasts beautifully with the pink shrimp and adds just the right amount of heat to the dish. If you don't have time to make your own pasta, use store-bought fettucine and add a chile or two to the sauce.

Pasta

1 teaspoon vegetable oil

6 jalapeño chiles, stemmed, seeded, and finely chopped (½ cup)

2 cups trimmed spinach leaves (about 4 ounces)

2 poblano chiles, roasted, peeled, seeded, and diced (½ cup)

2 eggs

1 tablespoon plus 1 teaspoon salt

2½ to 3 cups all-purpose flour

Shrimp and Sauce

2 tablespoons olive oil

1½ pounds large shrimp (26 to 30 per pound), peeled and deveined

4 cloves garlic, finely chopped

½ cup dry white wine

1 cup seeded and diced tomatoes

2 tablespoons finely chopped cilantro

Salt and freshly ground black pepper to taste

½ cup heavy cream

¾ cup grated cotija cheese (substitute goat or feta cheese)

Cilantro sprigs, for garnish

For the pasta: In a small skillet, heat the vegetable oil over medium-low heat. Add the jalapeños, cover, and cook until the chiles are softened, about 15 minutes. Fill a saucepan halfway with water and bring to a boil over high heat. Add the spinach and cook until bright green, about 1 minute. Drain and immediately plunge the spinach into ice water; drain and squeeze dry in paper towels or a clean dish towel. In the bowl of a food processor, place the cooked jalapeños, cooked spinach, and poblanos; purée. Add the eggs and 1 teaspoon of the salt and purée again. Add 2½ cups of the flour and pulse until a soft dough forms, adding more flour if necessary. Divide the dough into fourths, wrap in plastic wrap, and let it rest for about 30 minutes.

Unwrap one ball of dough at a time and, using a pasta machine, roll through setting 1 five or six times until the dough is smooth. Then roll through settings 2 through 6 one time each. Change the handle of the machine to the fettucine cutter and roll the dough through it. Hang the fettucine on the back of a chair or on a pasta drying rack while rolling out and cutting the remaining dough. In the meantime, bring a large pot of water to a rolling boil; add the remaining 1 tablespoon salt. Add cut fettucine and cook until al dente, about 3 minutes. Drain and reserve until the sauce is ready.

For the shrimp and sauce: In a large skillet, heat the olive oil over medium-high heat. Add the shrimp and garlic and cook until the shrimp just start to turn pink. Remove the shrimp and set aside. Add the wine, tomatoes, cilantro, salt, and pepper to the hot skillet and raise the heat to high. Bring to a boil, add the cream, and continue to cook until the sauce thickens, about 5 minutes. Add the pasta, shrimp, and cheese; toss together and cook until all the ingredients are warmed through, another 2 minutes. Immediately divide the pasta and shrimp among 6 warmed plates or shallow bowls and garnish with cilantro sprigs.

Lobster and Corn Enchiladas

Janos Wilder

Serves 4

This is a perfect example of modern Southwestern cuisine—elevating the lowly enchilada to haute cuisine with lobster.

Red Chile Velouté

1 tablespoon olive oil
1 tablespoon all-purpose flour
1 tablespoon tomato paste
2 teaspoons finely chopped garlic
1½ tablespoons chile powder
2 cups rich chicken stock
Salt and freshly ground black
   pepper to taste

Lobster-Corn Coulis

1½ cups lobster stock (substitute
   fish or vegetable stock)
2 teaspoons coarsely chopped
   garlic
2 cups fresh corn kernels cut
   from the cob (about 4 ears),
   cobs reserved
2 tablespoons anisette liqueur
2 tablespoons brandy
½ cup heavy cream

Enchiladas

1 tablespoon butter
½ cup corn kernels cut from the
   cob (about 1 ear)
8 ounces cooked lobster meat
2 cups grated white Cheddar
   cheese
2 poblano chiles, roasted,
   peeled, seeded, and diced
½ cup toasted pepitas (pumpkin
   seeds)
8 corn tortillas, 6 inches in
   diameter
½ cup chopped green onions,
   white and light green parts
½ cup Tomatillo Salsa (see
   page 200)

Do Ahead { The velouté and the coulis can be made a day ahead, covered, and refrigerated.

For the red chile velouté: Heat the olive oil in a saucepan over medium-high heat; when hot, add the flour and cook, whisking constantly, until the mixture turns dark brown, about 5 minutes. Whisk in the tomato paste, garlic, and chile powder. Slowly add the stock, whisking constantly until each addition is fully incorporated. After all the stock had been added, reduce the heat and simmer until the sauce is thickened, about 15 more minutes. Strain into a skillet. Season with salt and pepper and keep warm.

For the lobster-corn coulis: Place the stock, garlic, corn, reserved cobs, anisette liqueur, and brandy in a large saucepan and bring to a boil over high heat. Reduce the heat and simmer until the liquid is reduced by half (about ¾ cup remaining), 15 to 20 minutes. Add the cream and reduce until about 1 cup of liquid remains, 5 to 10 minutes more. Remove and discard the cobs. Let cool slightly and transfer to a blender; purée and strain into a clean saucepan. Season with salt and pepper to taste. Refrigerate if not using immediately and reheat just before serving.

For the enchilada filling: Preheat an oven to 400°. In a small skillet, heat the butter over medium heat. Add the corn and sauté for 2 to 3 minutes, until the corn is softened and has absorbed the butter. Turn the corn out into a large bowl. Add the lobster, 1 cup of the cheese, the chiles, and pepitas; toss well. Season with salt and pepper to taste.

Reheat the red chile velouté in a skillet over medium-low heat (do not get it too hot); dip a tortilla into the warm sauce and put on a plate. Spoon about ⅓ cup of filling into the center of the tortilla; roll the enchilada into a cylinder and place in an ovenproof casserole. Repeat with the remaining tortillas and filling. Pour the remaining velouté sauce over the enchiladas and sprinkle the remaining cup of cheese over all. Bake until heated through and the cheese is melted, 7 to 10 minutes. Sprinkle chopped green onions over the enchiladas.

Assembly: Place about ¼ cup lobster-corn coulis on each of 4 plates. Place 2 enchiladas on top and serve with tomatillo salsa.

Shrimp Enchiladas with Goat Cheese and Chipotle Cream

Vincent Guerithault · Serves 4

This would make an enticing main course for a special lunch or a casual gathering of friends late one Sunday morning. Pair it with a salad and you have modern Southwestern cuisine at its best.

1 cup diced leek, white and light green parts
½ cup heavy cream
4 ounces mild goat cheese
Salt and freshly ground black pepper to taste
1 teaspoon olive oil
12 shrimp (26 to 30 per pound), peeled and deveined

Chipotle Cream

2 chipotle chiles in adobo sauce
1 cup heavy cream

4 flour tortillas, 8 inches in diameter

Fill a saucepan halfway with water and bring to a boil over high heat. Add the leeks, cook about 1 minute, and immediately drain and rinse with cold water. Wipe the pan dry and return the leeks to the pan. Add cream, goat cheese, salt, and pepper. Place the pan over medium heat and cook, stirring, until the cheese is melted and the sauce is somewhat thickened, about 10 minutes. Set aside.

In a skillet, heat the olive oil over medium-high heat. When hot, add the shrimp and sauté until they just turn pink, 1 to 2 minutes. When cool enough to handle, slice the shrimp lengthwise along their backs so there are now 24 pieces of shrimp.

For the chipotle cream: In a mini food processor or with a sharp knife, very finely chop the chiles; strain into a small saucepan. (There should be about 1 tablespoon purée.) Add the cream to the pan and heat over medium heat, whisking, until the mixture is smooth and heated through.

Assembly: Preheat an oven to 350°. Divide the cheese-leek mixture evenly among 4 tortillas, placing the mixture along the length of the center of the tortillas. Place 4 shrimp pieces on top and roll up into a cylinder. Place in an 8 x 8-inch ovenproof dish and pour the chipotle cream over all; cover with foil. Heat in the oven until warmed through, 10 to 15 minutes. Remove from the oven and, with a spatula, place 1 enchilada on each plate. Top each with 2 pieces of the remaining shrimp and surround with a spoonful of the sauce from the bottom of the baking dish. Serve immediately.

Goat Cheese and Crab Rellenos with Fiery Black Bean–Pineapple Salsa

Stephan Pyles

Makes 10

Stephan prefers to "roast" the chiles for rellenos by frying them in hot oil for a few minutes until they blister. He then dips them in ice water, drains them, and peels off the skin, which crackles apart. They don't have the same depth of flavor as ones roasted over a flame, but Stephan's method keeps the flesh firm, better for stuffing.

Fiery Black Bean– Pineapple Salsa

¾ cup dried black beans

4 cups chicken stock

2 tablespoons freshly squeezed lime juice

1 habanero chile, seeded and minced

2 tablespoons diced mango

2 tablespoons diced pineapple

1 tablespoon diced red bell pepper

1 tablespoon diced yellow bell pepper

1 teaspoon chopped basil

1 teaspoon chopped cilantro

Salt to taste

Rellenos

10 large long green chiles (Anaheim or New Mexico), roasted, peeled, and stems left intact

1 head garlic, roasted (see page 214) and puréed

3 ounces mild goat cheese

¼ cup grated Monterey jack or Chihuahua cheese

1 pound jumbo lump crabmeat, cleaned of shells and cartilage

Do Ahead { The salsa can be made a day ahead, covered, and refrigerated. Before frying, the rellenos can be assembled up to 4 hours ahead and refrigerated.

For the salsa: In a saucepan, soak the black beans in 2 cups of the stock and refrigerate overnight. Remove the pan from the refrigerator; add the lime juice and bring the mixture to a boil over medium-high heat. Reduce the heat and simmer until the beans are just tender, about 45 minutes, adding more liquid if necessary. Remove the pan from the heat and strain the beans. Measure and set aside ¾ cup beans. Place the remaining beans and the remaining 2 cups chicken stock in a blender and purée until smooth; pour back into the saucepan. Add the reserved beans and remaining ingredients. Heat over low heat until warmed through.

For the rellenos: Carefully slit the chiles down one side and remove the seeds, leaving the stems attached. In a large mixing bowl, combine the garlic, goat cheese, grated cheese, crab, shallot, roasted bell peppers, herbs, and 2 tablespoons of the pepitas. Season with salt and pepper to taste; mix well. Stuff the chiles with the mixture, being careful not to overfill. Pulling the slit together, close the chiles and refrigerate for at least 30 minutes before frying.

In a heavy saucepan, heat at least 2 inches of peanut oil to 325°. In a shallow bowl or rimmed plate, beat the egg into the cream. In another plate, place the seasoned cornmeal. To coat each relleno, first roll

1 tablespoon chopped shallot
2 tablespoons diced roasted red
  bell pepper
2 tablespoons diced roasted
  yellow bell pepper
1 tablespoon chopped cilantro
1 tablespoon chopped basil
1 tablespoon chopped marjoram
¼ cup coarsely chopped roasted
  pepitas (pumpkin seeds)
Salt and freshly ground black
  pepper to taste

4 cups peanut oil for frying
1 egg
2 tablespoons heavy cream
2 cups yellow cornmeal mixed
  with 2 teaspoons salt for
  dredging
Three-Tomato Pico (see
  page 199)
8 sprigs cilantro, for garnish

in the egg mixture, then in the cornmeal. Gently drop 1 or 2 rellenos at a time into the hot oil and fry until lightly browned, about 3 to 5 minutes. Remove from the oil and drain on paper towels.

Assembly: Ladle about ⅓ cup bean sauce onto each serving plate. Place a relleno next to the sauce and top with 2 tablespoons three-tomato pico. Garnish the plate with a cilantro sprig and some of the remaining 2 tablespoons toasted pepitas.

 The black bean salsa features the fiery habanero chile. On a 1 to 10 scale, it's about a 17. One habanero is more than enough for a whole recipe. Handle it with care. It is 50 times hotter than a jalapeño.

Lobster, Tomato, and Basil Rellenos

John Rivera Sedlar

**Serves 8 as an appetizer
or 4 as a main course**

When your tomatoes are ripe on the vine in summer, and basil is lush and green, it's time to harvest the crop to make these elegant rellenos from the master of modern Southwestern cooking.

1 slice white bread, crust removed

1 pound cooked lobster meat (1 large Maine lobster or 2 lobster tails)

1 cup seeded and diced tomato

2 tablespoons thinly sliced fresh basil leaves

3 tablespoons extra virgin olive oil

1 teaspoon salt, plus salt to taste

1 teaspoon freshly ground black pepper

8 Anaheim chiles, roasted and peeled

Butter Sauce (see page 26)

Do Ahead { The rellenos can be stuffed up to 4 hours ahead, covered, and refrigerated.

Preheat an oven to 350°.

Place the bread in the bowl of a food processor and pulse until crumbled; turn crumbs out into a bowl. Add the lobster, tomato, basil, olive oil, salt, and pepper. Refrigerate, covered, if not using immediately.

With the tip of a small, sharp knife, slice each chile open lengthwise from the base of its stem to the tip, leaving the stem attached. Open flat and remove the seeds and ribs. Lightly salt the inside of each chile.

With a teaspoon, neatly mound the filling in the center of each chile, distributing it evenly. Pull the slit together to close the sides around the filling.

Place the chiles, seam sides down, on a baking sheet. Bake until warmed through, about 15 minutes. Remove from the oven and put 1 relleno in the center of each plate for a first course or 2 rellenos in the center of each plate for a main course. Drizzle with butter sauce and sprinkle any leftover filling on top and around the rellenos. Serve immediately.

Blue Corn–Crusted Cabrilla with Rainbow Posole Broth

Janos Wilder   Serves 4

Posole, another name for hominy, is corn that has been treated with an alkaline substance to remove the hard outer shell. The colored posoles in this recipe are made from red, blue, and white corn. White and yellow hominy are available in most supermarkets, but you can special-order the colored heirlooms from Native Seeds/SEARCH (see Mail-Order Sources, page 217).

Rainbow Posole Broth

2 tablespoons vegetable oil
1 cup diced carrots
1 cup diced onions
1 cup diced celery
3 tablespoons minced garlic
½ cup fresh oregano, finely
   chopped
4 cups rich chicken stock
½ cup cooked red posole
½ cup cooked blue posole
½ cup cooked white posole
Salt and freshly ground black
   pepper to taste

Fish

¾ cup ground blue corn chips
   (about 4 ounces)
3 tablespoons chile powder
Salt and freshly ground black
   pepper to taste
4 cabrilla fillets (7 ounces each)
4 tablespoons unsalted butter,
   clarified

Salsa Fresca (see page 198)
4 wedges lime
¼ cup cilantro leaves

For the rainbow posole broth: In a large saucepan, heat the 2 tablespoons vegetable oil over medium heat. Add the carrots, onions, and celery and sauté until softened, about 10 minutes. Add the garlic and oregano and cook another minute. Add the chicken stock and posole. Season with salt and pepper to taste. Cook until heated through, about 5 more minutes.

For the fish: Preheat an oven to 400°. In a shallow dish, stir together the corn chips, chile powder, salt, and pepper. Roll the fillets in the mixture until thoroughly coated.

In a large, ovenproof skillet, heat the butter over medium heat. When hot, add the fillets and sear on both sides until lightly browned, about 1 minute per side. Transfer the pan to the oven and cook the fillets until cooked through, 6 to 8 minutes.

Place ¾ cup of the posole broth in each of 4 shallow bowls. Place a fish fillet in the center of each bowl and garnish with Salsa Fresca, lime wedges, and cilantro leaves.

 Each color of posole has a different cooking time: the white cooks the fastest (about 1½ hours), the blue takes about 2 hours, and the red takes the longest—2½ to 3 hours—so plan accordingly. They'll start to pop when they're done. To test: Take one out of the water and cut in half. If it's cooked and puffed, it's done. If the center is still white and powdery, cook longer.

Pan~Fried Canyon Trout

Robert McGrath

Serves 4

Fresh-caught trout cooked over a campfire. What a treat! Robert hooked one in Oak Creek, but it couldn't wait for the camera to record the catch. So we used our "reserve" from the local supermarket. The cornmeal coating adds great flavor and texture to the fish, at the same time keeping it moist.

2 cups yellow cornmeal

2 teaspoons salt

1 teaspoon freshly ground black pepper

2 tablespoons vegetable shortening

4 boneless rainbow trout, cut in half lengthwise (8 pieces)

Salad of Spring Melons and Green Onions (see page 45)

1 bunch chives (about 20), for garnish

4 wedges lime, for garnish

Combine cornmeal, salt, and pepper in a shallow dish or plate large enough to hold a piece of trout.

Heat a cast-iron skillet over hot coals or over medium-high heat. When the pan is hot, add the vegetable shortening and allow to melt.

One at a time, coat both sides of each piece of trout with the cornmeal mixture; gently add to the hot pan. Cook in batches if necessary (do not crowd the pan). Cook until lightly browned and crisp on one side, about 2 minutes; turn over and cook the other side, 2 more minutes.

Spoon about 1 cup of the salad into the center of each of 4 plates. Spoon some of the liquid from the salad around the perimeter of the plates. Top each portion with 2 pieces of cooked trout; squeeze a lime wedge over each portion of trout and garnish with whole chives. Serve immediately.

Cast iron is mandatory for cooking outdoors. A campfire gets hot, but the heat doesn't last very long. Cast-iron skillets and Dutch ovens retain and distribute heat beautifully, which is why they're such a favorite. Besides, they give food some soul.

Cornmeal~Crusted Sea Bass with Corn and Tomatillo Salsa

Serves 4

Although the fish isn't from the Southwest, giving it a cornmeal coat and serving it with a corn and tomatillo salsa makes it an honorary Southwestern ingredient.

Salsa

1 ear corn

6 tomatillos, husked and washed

⅓ cup seeded and diced tomato

1 jalapeño chile, seeded and diced

⅓ cup seeded and diced cucumber

⅓ cup chopped red onion

⅓ cup diced red bell pepper

2 tablespoons chopped cilantro

1 tablespoon freshly squeezed lime juice

1 teaspoons salt

Freshly ground black pepper to taste

Sea Bass

2 tablespoons olive oil

½ cup buttermilk

½ cup cornmeal

4 fillets of sea bass, red snapper, or catfish (4 ounces each)

Salt and freshly ground black pepper to taste

Do Ahead { The salsa can be made up to 4 hours ahead, covered, and refrigerated. Bring back to room temperature before serving.

For the salsa: Roast the corn over an open flame, on a barbecue grill, or under a broiler until just browned. When cool, cut the kernels from the cob. Put the kernels in a bowl and set aside. Place the tomatillos in a small saucepan and cover with water. Bring to a boil, reduce the heat, and simmer until soft, about 5 minutes. Drain and purée in a blender until smooth. Pour into the bowl containing the corn and add the diced tomato, jalapeño, cucumber, onion, red pepper, cilantro, lime juice, salt, and pepper. Set aside.

For the sea bass: In a large skillet, heat the olive oil over medium heat. Pour the buttermilk into a shallow dish and sprinkle the cornmeal into another one. Season the fish fillets with salt and pepper to taste; dip into the buttermilk, then dredge in the cornmeal. Sauté the fish until lightly browned, 3 to 4 minutes per side. Transfer to warm plates and serve with the room-temperature salsa on the side.

8 ounces yellowfin tuna (sashimi quality; loin approximately 2 x 2-inch diameter)

1½ teaspoons olive oil

½ teaspoon olive oil

¼ teaspoon freshly squeezed lemon juice

1½ cups *frisée* and mizuna lettuce

¼ teaspoon salt

In a small bowl, whisk together the remaining ½ teaspoon olive oil and the lemon juice. Put the greens into a bowl and toss with salt. Add the oil-lemon mixture and toss well.

Assembly: Place 3 tablespoons of beans in the center of each of four 10-inch plates. Around each serving of beans drizzle 1½ teaspoons cilantro purée and ½ teaspoon balsamic syrup. Divide the greens among 4 plates, placing greens on top of the beans. Cut the tuna into 12 equal pieces; on each plate, fan 3 pieces on the top of the greens. Serve immediately.

Southwest Omelet

Vincent Guerithault

Serves 2

This classic French *omelet aux fines herbes* reflects Vincent's background in classic cuisine. But he moved to Arizona and his cooking did, too. The addition of tortillas reflects this fortuitous change of direction.

2 slices bacon

1 tablespoon unsalted butter

3 eggs

3 tablespoons water

1 teaspoon finely chopped fresh basil

1 teaspoon finely chopped cilantro or fresh parsley

Salt and freshly ground black pepper to taste

1 flour tortilla, 8 inches in diameter

In an 8-inch skillet, cook the bacon over medium-high heat until crisp and browned, about 5 minutes. Remove the bacon, drain on a paper towel, and set aside. Discard any bacon grease left in the pan and wipe the pan clean. Add the butter to the pan and place over medium heat. In a small bowl, beat together the eggs, water, herbs, salt, and pepper. Add the egg mixture to the hot skillet and cook, lifting the sides as it cooks to allow uncooked eggs to flow to the bottom of the pan, until the omelet is set, 3 to 5 minutes. Flip the omelet onto the tortilla. Roll up and slice into 6 pieces. Arrange 3 slices on each of 2 plates and arrange the bacon on top.

To fill the tortilla completely with omelet, be sure both omelet and tortilla are the same diameter.

Fiesta Brunch Casserole

Serves 6 to 8

Perfect for out-of-town house guests, this one-dish meal can be assembled the night before and served to company the next morning. What a way to introduce newcomers to the flavors of the Southwest.

2 tablespoons unsalted butter, melted

5 flour tortillas, 8 inches in diameter

1 package (12 ounces) hot breakfast sausage, crumbled

1 cup diced red bell pepper (about 1 large pepper)

1 cup diced yellow bell pepper (about 1 large pepper)

1 cup finely chopped green onions (about 8 green onions, white and light green parts)

1 large clove garlic, finely chopped

1 jalapeño chile, stemmed, seeded, and finely chopped

8 eggs

⅓ cup milk

½ teaspoon chili powder

½ teaspoon salt

2 cups grated Monterey jack cheese

Cilantro leaves, for garnish

Sour cream

1½ cups Salsa Fresca (see page 198)

Do Ahead { You can assemble the casserole the night before, cover tightly with plastic wrap, and refrigerate.

Lightly brush the inside of an 8-inch springform pan with the melted butter. Brush both sides of the tortillas with the remaining melted butter. Center 1 tortilla in the bottom of the pan. Arrange the remaining tortillas around the sides of pan, overlapping slightly, allowing about 2 inches overhang and covering the pan completely. Set the pan on a baking sheet.

Preheat an oven to 350°.

Heat a heavy skillet over medium-high heat and add the sausage. Cook until browned, crumbling with a fork, and spoon off the excess fat. Reduce the heat to medium and add the bell peppers. Cook until tender, about 5 minutes. Add the chopped green onions, garlic, and jalapeño and cook another 2 minutes. Remove from the heat. Spread the sausage mixture evenly over the tortillas, gently pressing the tortillas to conform to the sides of the pan.

In a large bowl, whisk together the eggs, milk, chili powder, and salt. Set aside. Heat the same heavy skillet in which the sausage was cooked over medium heat. Add the egg mixture and cook, stirring, just until the eggs begin to set, about 5 minutes; do not overcook. Remove from the heat.

Sprinkle 1 cup of the cheese over the sausage mixture. Spoon the scrambled eggs over the cheese and top with the remaining 1 cup of cheese. Fold the tortilla overhang over the cheese. Bake until lightly browned and warmed through, about 30 minutes. Let stand 5 minutes. Run a thin knife between the tortillas and the pan sides; release the sides. Garnish with cilantro leaves and serve hot with sour cream and salsa.

Chapter 5

Vegetables

When the Spanish came here looking for gold, they didn't find it. But they brought a culinary treasure that may be even more valuable—fresh chiles, the signature ingredient of the Southwest.

As they moved north, the Spanish took chiles with them into New Mexico. But like almost everything about the region, chiles get their vitality from many sources. Another ancestor is certainly the fiery, wild chiltepín that still flourishes in Arizona, New Mexico, and Texas. This tiny red pod was collected and eaten long before the European explorers ever set foot in the New World.

For hundreds of years after the Spanish arrived, chile cultivation was a matter of chance. But in the 1950s agriculturalists in New Mexico (some view the state as one big outdoor chile laboratory) tamed the chile, transferring it from an out-of-control ball of fire to a multipurpose, reproducible vegetable. New Mexico celebrates its most famous crop every fall with a festival in the tiny Rio Grande Valley town of Hatch, dubbed the Chile Capital of the World.

Although chiles are all about heat—produced by the compound capsaicin stored in the ribs and seeds—all chiles are not created equal. Size does matter, but in reverse: Larger chiles like the poblano can be earthy, fruity, and relatively mild. On the other end of the ruler, the pint-sized, incendiary orb, the habanero, is rated the hottest chile in the world—200,000 units on the Scoville chile scale (poblanos barely simmer at 1,000 units).

If eating chiles can be painful—they scorch our mouth and throat and make us sweat—why do we love them so? Is it the taste? They are a wonderful flavor enhancer. Do we eat them for our health? Green chiles do have twice as much vitamin C as citrus. And capsaicin has been used as a cure-all for everything from indigestion to arthritis. Are they the spice of life? Recent university studies have shown that chiles can knock out up to 75 percent of certain food-borne germs.

Most likely, we eat chiles for the thrill of it. Scientists say that chiles give us the same endorphin rush we get from jumping off a cliff tied to a stretchy bungee cord, or from screaming down a snow-covered ski slope. They've even give the experience a name: mouth-surfing.

Come try this new culinary sport, perfected by such chile experts as Stephan Pyles. His Goat Cheese and Crab Rellenos with Fiery Black Bean–Pineapple Salsa (see page 108) invests traditional chile rellenos with a bit of culinary hellfire in the form of the fierce habanero.

This chapter features innovative vegetable side dishes that are packed with chiles from sedate to sizzling. Among them are Robert McGrath's Green Chile Macaroni (see page 143), a lively Wild West version of humble Sunday supper fare, and Janos Wilder's Exotic Mushroom and Smoked Poblano Flan (see page 138), a certain menu-maker.

Asparagus with Cactus~ Chile Glaze

Serves 6 to 8

The sweet fruit of the cactus gives prickly pear marmalade its ruby hue. The spread is available in many markets in the Southwest, but may be difficult to find in other parts of the country. A good orange marmalade or currant jelly are fine substitutes. This casual vegetable side dish complements any sauceless main course, particularly grilled meat, chicken, or fish.

1 teaspoon salt
2 bunches asparagus (about 2 pounds)
4 tablespoons unsalted butter
1 tablespoon finely chopped shallot
1 jalapeño chile, finely chopped
2 tablespoons tequila
½ cup freshly squeezed orange juice
¼ cup prickly pear marmalade (substitute orange marmalade)
Salt and freshly ground black pepper to taste
¼ cup toasted piñon nuts (substitute pine nuts)

Do Ahead { The asparagus can be cooked a few hours ahead. The glaze can be made a day ahead, covered, and refrigerated, then brought back to a boil before adding the asparagus.

Fill a large sauté pan with water and add 1 teaspoon salt; bring to a boil. Add the asparagus and cook until just tender, 5 to 8 minutes. Immediately put the asparagus in ice water to refresh; drain on paper towels.

Wipe the sauté pan dry and place over medium heat. Add 1 tablespoon of the unsalted butter to the pan and, when melted, add the shallot and jalapeño. Cook until tender, 2 to 3 minutes. Add the tequila, orange juice, prickly pear marmalade, and the remaining 3 tablespoons butter to the pan; bring to a boil. Boil until slightly thickened, about 2 minutes.

Season the asparagus with salt and pepper to taste; add to the sauté pan and heat gently, turning to coat with the orange glaze. Remove to a platter or individual plates and sprinkle with piñon nuts. Serve warm as a side dish or at room temperature as a salad.

Select firm, bright-green asparagus with tightly closed tips and not much white stalk. Snap off the end of the stem, then remove any tough skin with a vegetable peeler or paring knife.

Zesty Zucchini

Serves 4 to 6

You'll never go back to bland zucchini after trying this version. The Green Chile and Tomatillo Sauce adds a kick and enhances the natural green color of the zucchini, but to save time, you could substitute bottled salsa.

2 large or 3 medium zucchini
1 tablespoon olive oil
¼ cup chopped green onions
2 cloves garlic, peeled and finely chopped
¼ cup Green Chile and Tomatillo Sauce (see page 195)
Salt and freshly ground black pepper to taste

Cut the zucchini into ⅛-inch slices. In a large skillet, heat the olive oil over medium heat. Add the zucchini, green onions, and garlic; sauté until the vegetables are barely tender but still bright green, about 5 minutes. Add the green chile and tomatillo sauce and season with salt and pepper to taste. Cook until the mixture is warmed through. Serve immediately.

Skillet Corn Cake

Loretta Barrett Oden   Serves 6 to 8

This was one of Loretta's favorite childhood dishes, but back then bacon drippings and crumbled bacon were part of the recipe. This is her updated, healthier version that's lost some fat, but none of its goodness.

⅓ cup corn oil
8 to 10 medium ears fresh corn, cut into kernels, or 4 to 5 cups thawed frozen or drained canned corn kernels
½ cup finely chopped onion
2 tablespoons seeded and finely chopped serrano or jalapeño chile
⅓ cup all-purpose flour
Salt and freshly ground black pepper to taste
Tomato Preserves (see page 204) or Salsa Fresca (see page 198)

Preheat an oven to 425°. Place the corn oil in a 10-inch ovenproof skillet (preferably cast-iron) and heat in the oven until very hot, 15 to 20 minutes.

In a large bowl, combine the corn, onion, chile, flour, salt, and pepper. Transfer the corn mixture to the skillet and press firmly into the hot oil to compact; smooth the top. Return the pan to the oven and cook until a brown crust forms on the bottom of the corn cake, 25 to 30 minutes. Remove from the oven and loosen the sides with a spatula. Invert a serving plate over the top of the skillet, then invert the skillet onto the plate so that the browned side of the corn cake is showing. Cut into wedges and serve hot with tomato preserves or salsa fresca.

Medley of Corn, Squash, Tomatoes, and Chiles

Serves 6

In view of today's focus on a healthy diet with plentiful amounts of fresh vegetables, it might seem that vegetable dishes like this one are newly invented. But in fact, corn, squash, tomatoes, and chiles, all indigenous to the Americas, possess an ancient lineage.

Salsa

2 medium ripe tomatoes, finely chopped

¼ cup finely chopped onion

1 serrano chile, stemmed, seeded, and finely chopped

1 tablespoon finely chopped cilantro

½ teaspoon sugar

1 tablespoon freshly squeezed lime juice

Salt and freshly ground pepper to taste

1 tablespoon unsalted butter

1 tablespoon olive oil

3 cups corn kernels

1 cup diced zucchini or other summer squash

½ cup green onions, white and light green parts, chopped

Salt and freshly ground black pepper to taste

1 tablespoon fresh oregano leaves

Do Ahead { The salsa can be made without the cilantro up to 4 hours ahead. Add the cilantro just before using.

For the salsa: In a nonreactive medium bowl, combine all the salsa ingredients; set aside.

In a large skillet, melt the butter and olive oil over medium heat. When hot, add the corn, squash, and green onions. Add salt and pepper to taste and cook until the vegetables are tender, about 5 minutes. Add the salsa and continue to cook until warmed through, about 5 more minutes. Adjust the seasonings to taste, sprinkle with oregano leaves, and serve immediately, or cool to room temperature and serve as a salad.

For an unusual—but very appropriate—presentation, serve this dish in corn husk boats (see corn husks, page 214).

Corn Cooked in Husks on the Grill

Serves 6

This very simple—but oh-so-good—dish depends on the best fresh corn for success. Buy the corn the day you use it from a local farmers' market. To ready the ears for grilling, the corn is freed of its silk, rewrapped in its husk, and soaked so the husk doesn't burn when exposed to the fire. The chile butter is also great as a spread for a spicy bread or as a baste for chicken.

6 ears corn in their husks

Chile-Lime Butter

4 tablespoons unsalted butter, softened

2 teaspoons chile powder

2 teaspoons fresh lime juice

Salt and freshly ground black pepper to taste

Do Ahead { Chile-lime butter can be made up to 2 days ahead, covered, and refrigerated. Bring back to room temperature before brushing on the corn.

Preheat a gas grill or light a charcoal fire.

Pull the husks back from the corn and remove the silks; pull the husks back into place around the corn. Soak the ears in warm water for at least 30 minutes.

For the chile-lime butter: In a small bowl, whisk together the butter, chile powder, lime juice, salt, and pepper.

Remove the corn from the water and pat dry. Gently peel the husks back from the corn and brush the corn with the butter. Pull the husks back around the corn, and tie with a piece of husk or kitchen string to keep the husks around the corn.

When the grill is hot enough, place the cobs on the rack and cook until the kernels are tender and lightly browned, about 20 minutes, turning occasionally. The outer husks will burn, but the inner layers will protect the corn. Remove husks and serve immediately. Pass additional chile-lime butter.

 Use only freshly squeezed lime juice when mixing up the chile butter. Its tartness kicks up the flavor of the chile and pairs well with the sweetness of the corn.

Broccoli and Red Bell Peppers in Chile Butter

Serves 6

When exposed to chile power in the form of earthy, dark green poblanos, even much-maligned broccoli takes on new gusto. Sweet bell peppers are roasted in the same way as chiles (see page 213) and for the same reason—for a deeper, sweeter flavor and to remove their bitter skin.

3 cups broccoli florets

4 tablespoons unsalted butter

½ teaspoon cumin seed, toasted and ground

1 cup diced tomatoes

2 poblano chiles, roasted, peeled, seeded, and diced

2 red bell peppers, roasted, peeled, seeded, and cut into strips

Salt and freshly ground black pepper to taste

Fill a Dutch oven or large pot halfway with water and bring to a boil over high heat. Add the broccoli and cook until just tender, about 5 minutes. Plunge the broccoli immediately into ice water; drain and reserve.

Wipe the Dutch oven dry and place over medium heat; add the butter. When the butter melts, add the cumin, tomatoes, and chiles and cook, stirring, for 1 to 2 minutes. Add the broccoli and red pepper strips, toss, and cook, covered, until heated through, 3 to 5 minutes. Season with salt and pepper to taste and serve immediately.

Sauté of Chayote Squash

Serves 6

Chayote, also known as vegetable pear, is a tropical summer squash with a mild flavor that nicely shows off spicy ingredients. It's widely available, but if you can't find it, use yellow squash or zucchini instead. Serve this simple sauté with grilled fish, poultry, or meat, garnished with sprigs of cilantro.

1 tablespoon olive oil

1 serrano chile, stemmed, seeded, and finely chopped

¼ cup finely chopped red onion

3 chayote squash, peeled and thinly sliced

Salt and freshly ground black pepper to taste

2 tablespoons finely chopped cilantro

Heat the olive oil in a large, heavy skillet over medium heat. Add the serrano and onion and cook, stirring, for 1 minute. Add the squash and season with salt and pepper to taste. Cover, reduce the heat, and cook until the squash is just tender. Remove the cover and add the cilantro. Taste and add more salt and pepper if necessary.

Cactus Fries

Jay McCarthy

Serves 4

The creation of "Cactus King" Jay McCarthy, these are no ordinary spuds. He takes strips of cactus pads—nopales—and dips them in a batter infused with the pink color and sweet taste of prickly pear purée. Serve them as an appetizer, side dish, or even as a first course topped with shrimp or scallops. Cactus pads taste a bit like green beans crossed with okra. For these fries, use only fresh cactus pads, available at Latino markets and in many supermarkets in the Southwest, not those sold preserved in jars.

2 pounds prickly pear cactus pads (nopales)

3 tablespoons cornstarch

2 tablespoons Achiote Paste (see page 205)

⅔ cup all-purpose flour

1 teaspoon baking powder

1 egg white

About ¾ cup ice water

Peanut oil for frying

Salsa or ketchup, for accompaniment

With a sharp paring knife, remove the thorns and "eyes" from the cactus pads; trim the edges of the pads. Bring a large pot of salted water to a boil over high heat; reduce heat, add pads, cover, and simmer for 2 minutes; drain. Cut the cactus pads into 3- to 4-inch strips about the size of French fries. Set aside.

Combine the cornstarch and achiote paste in a blender or food processor; pulse until smooth. Turn into a bowl. Add the flour and baking powder; mix well. In another bowl, whisk the egg white until stiff peaks form. Add half of the flour mixture to the egg white and fold in. Add half the ice water, then the remaining flour mixture and enough water to make the batter the consistency of beaten egg white. Refrigerate the batter until chilled, about 20 to 30 minutes.

Fill a heavy skillet with enough peanut oil to a depth of 2 inches. Heat the oil over medium-high heat to 375°. Remove the batter from the refrigerator and, one at a time, dip the cactus strips in it. Drop the strips into the hot oil and cook until crispy and golden, 2 to 3 minutes. Drain on paper towels and serve immediately with salsa or ketchup.

So the fries don't clump as they cook, drop them into the hot oil one by one. And don't put too many in at one time; this lowers the heat and they won't be as crispy. They're done when the batter is light brown and the bubbles around each strip are almost gone.

Seared Chard

Mary Sue Milliken and Susan Feniger

Serves 4

Keep the pan really hot when you sear the greens because it cools down quickly each time more ingredients are added, instruct the chefs. If you're cooking a pile of greens, do it in several batches.

2 bunches red or green Swiss chard or any other greens
2 tablespoons unsalted butter
2 tablespoons extra virgin olive oil
Salt and freshly ground black pepper to taste

Trim and discard the stems of the greens; wash and dry the leaves. Stack the leaves, roll into cylinders, and cut across the rolls into 1-inch strips.

In a large skillet over medium-high heat, melt 1 tablespoon of the butter; add 1 tablespoon of the olive oil. When hot, add half the greens and salt and pepper to taste; sauté until the greens are limp, 30 seconds to 1 minute. If the greens begin to brown before they wilt, sprinkle in a few drops of water to create steam. Transfer to a covered platter and repeat the procedure with the remaining greens. Serve immediately.

Wash greens thoroughly before you cook them to remove all the dirt. Fill the sink with cold water, and let gravity do the work: Pick up the greens from the water, give them a shake, and let the dirt fall to the bottom of the sink. Don't worry if any water still clings to the greens; it will help steam them.

White Grits with Bitter Greens

Robert Del Grande

Serves 4 to 6

Texas shares a border with Louisiana, so it's no surprise to see the Southern staple, grits, in a dish created by a Houston chef. Grits are ground hominy—processed dried corn with hull and germ removed. Most supermarkets stock it in the cereal aisle, next to oatmeal.

4 cups water
1½ teaspoons salt
1¼ cups coarse white grits
1 tablespoon unsalted butter
¾ cup finely chopped yellow
  onion
2 cloves garlic, finely chopped
4 ounces arugula or other bitter
  green, coarsely chopped
  (about ½ cup)
Salt and freshly ground black
  pepper to taste

In a heavy-bottomed 2-quart saucepan, bring the water to a boil. Add the salt. Gradually add the grits, stirring constantly. Bring the water back to a boil, then reduce the heat to a very low simmer. Cover the pan, but stir every 2 or 3 minutes until the grits are thick, about 20 minutes. If the grits become too thick, add a little more water to adjust the consistency.

In a skillet, melt the butter until foaming over medium-high heat. Add the onion and garlic; sauté until the onion is translucent, about 5 minutes. Add the greens and briefly sauté until wilted. Remove from the heat.

Just before serving, stir the greens into the grits. Add salt and pepper to taste and serve immediately.

Black Bean Cakes

Black Beans (see page 141)
Sour cream
Salsa Fresca (see page 198)

Place cooled, leftover black beans in the bowl of a food processor; purée until smooth. Heat a skillet over medium-high heat; spray with nonstick cooking spray. With a small ladle or large spoon, drop about 2 tablespoons bean purée per cake into the hot skillet; flatten with the back of a spatula. Cook until lightly browned, about 1 to 2 minutes; turn over and cook other side. Remove from the skillet and top each cake with a tablespoon of sour cream and a tablespoon of salsa fresca.

Gratin of Swiss Chard

Robert Del Grande   **Serves 4 to 6**

Chard is sturdier than spinach, according to chef Robert Del Grande, which is why he prefers it for this tasty casserole. Unlike spinach, chard holds up better when cooked, with more texture, and won't wilt down from a lot to very little.

At Cafe Annie in Houston, Robert serves it alongside Coffee-Roasted Fillet of Beef with Pasilla Chile Broth (see page 82). The sweetness of the fennel is a nice foil to the heat of the chile sauce.

2 bunches Swiss chard (about 1 pound each), thick stems removed and discarded
1 tablespoon unsalted butter
4 slices bacon, cut into small pieces
1 fennel bulb (about 1 pound), white part only, finely chopped
¼ cup chicken stock
Salt to taste
1 cup grated Monterey jack cheese

Do Ahead { The swiss chard casserole can be made a day ahead and refrigerated. Bring to room temperature before adding the cheese and heating in the oven.

Coarsely chop the Swiss chard leaves and set aside. In a large skillet over medium-high heat, melt the butter; add the bacon and sauté until lightly browned, about 5 minutes. Add the chopped fennel and sauté until slightly softened, 5 to 10 minutes. Raise the heat to high; when the skillet is very hot, add the Swiss chard pieces, a portion at a time, until all the leaves are wilted. Slowly add the chicken stock and salt to taste. Cook until the chicken stock has almost evaporated, another 5 to 10 minutes. Remove the pan from the heat and transfer the mixture to a shallow casserole dish.

Preheat an oven to 350°. Sprinkle the cheese over the Swiss chard mixture and bake until heated through and the cheese is melted, 10 to 15 minutes.

Roasted Pepper and Onion Tart

Serves 8

If this tart seems vaguely familiar, you might have tasted its French cousin—the quiche. But like all transplants to the Southwest, that rustic pastry quickly went native with such regional staples as masa harina, chiles, and cilantro.

Crust

- 1 teaspoon ancho chile powder or chile powder
- ½ cup masa harina
- ½ cup all-purpose flour
- 4 tablespoons unsalted butter
- ½ teaspoon salt
- 1 egg
- 2 to 3 tablespoons ice water

Filling

- 2 tablespoons olive oil
- 1½ cups chopped white onion
- 1 red bell pepper, roasted, seeded, peeled, and diced
- 1 yellow bell pepper, roasted, seeded, peeled, and diced
- 1 Anaheim chile, roasted, seeded, peeled, and diced
- 2 tablespoons chopped cilantro
- 1 head roasted garlic (see page 214)
- ¾ cup whipping cream
- 3 large eggs
- Salt and freshly ground pepper to taste

For the crust: In the bowl of a food processor, place the chile powder, masa harina, flour, butter, and salt. Pulse until the butter is in pea-sized pieces. Add the egg and pulse again. With the motor running, dribble in the cold water until the mixture starts to come together. Do not overprocess. Turn the mixture out onto a board and press together into a round disc. Wrap in plastic wrap and refrigerate for at least 1 hour or overnight.

Preheat an oven to 425°. On a floured surface, roll out the dough into either a 12-inch circle or a 15 x 11-inch rectangle. Turn the circle of dough into a 9-inch tart pan with a removable bottom or the rectangle of dough into an 11 x 7-inch rectangular pan. Prick the bottom of the dough with the back of a fork, cover with foil, and weight with dried beans, rice, or pie weights. Bake for 10 minutes. Remove the foil and weights and bake until light brown, about 10 more minutes. Remove the tart shell from the oven and let cool. Reduce the oven temperature to 400°.

For the filling: In a large skillet, heat the olive oil over medium heat. Add the onion and sauté until translucent and just beginning to brown, 10 to 15 minutes. Remove from the heat and let cool. Sprinkle the onion over the bottom of the baked crust. Top with the peppers, chile, and cilantro. Squeeze the softened cloves garlic from the roasted bulb into a blender. Add the cream, eggs, salt, and pepper and purée. Pour the liquid mixture over the vegetables in the crust. Bake in the oven until the custard sets, about 25 minutes. Allow to sit for 5 minutes and cut into 8 wedges for a first course or 32 squares for an appetizer. Serve warm or at room temperature.

 If you have trouble rolling out the dough, put it between two pieces of waxed paper, parchment paper, or plastic wrap and it won't stick. For easy transfer to the quiche pan, remove the top layer of paper and flip the dough over into the mold.

Exotic Mushroom and Smoked Poblano Flan

Janos Wilder

Serves 6

This creamy custard makes a delicious accompaniment to meat or poultry, but is also superb served on its own as a first course. It looks plain, but surprises the mouth with lots of flash and dash. Most well-stocked supermarkets, and certainly specialty produce stores, now sell a tempting collection of exotic mushrooms alongside the familiar white and brown buttons.

½ cup olive oil

1 tablespoon chopped garlic

Salt and freshly ground black pepper to taste

12 ounces portobello, shiitake, chanterelle, or other mushrooms, cleaned

2 poblano chiles, roasted, peeled, seeded, and diced

2 long green (Anaheim) chiles, roasted, peeled, seeded, and diced

2 whole eggs

1 cup heavy cream

12 strips roasted red bell pepper, for garnish (optional)

6 sprigs fresh herbs (rosemary, chervil, cilantro, parsley, or marjoram), for garnish (optional)

Preheat a gas grill or light a charcoal fire. In a bowl, combine the olive oil, garlic, salt, and pepper. Remove the stems from the mushrooms and discard. Add the mushroom caps to the oil mixture. Let marinate 15 to 20 minutes. Remove the mushrooms from the marinade and grill until browned, about 3 minutes, turning frequently. Let cool slightly.

Place the mushrooms and chiles in a food processor and pulse until chopped. Add the eggs and purée the mixture. With the machine running, slowly add the cream.

Preheat an oven to 375°. Butter six 4-ounce ramekins or timbales. Divide the mushroom-egg mixture among the ramekins. Place the ramekins in a baking pan and fill the pan halfway up the sides with water. Bake until set, about 25 minutes. Remove the ramekins from the water bath, unmold, and serve warm. Garnish the top of each flan with 2 strips of roasted red bell pepper and a sprig of fresh herb, if desired.

Chipotle Mashed Potatoes

Serves 6 to 8

The smokiness of the chipotle chile gives potatoes a unique flavor. Using a food mill or potato ricer ensures the creamy texture that is the hallmark of great mashed potatoes. Chipotles are partially dried, smoked jalapeños, so they can be quite hot. The Chipotle Mashed Potato Cakes are themselves a spectacular side dish.

2 teaspoons salt

4 pounds potatoes (preferably Yukon Gold), peeled and cut into 1-inch pieces

1 tablespoon olive oil

2 tablespoons finely chopped garlic

1 chipotle chile in adobo sauce, puréed

¾ cup milk, warmed

½ cup butter, at room temperature, cut in chunks

Salt and freshly ground black pepper to taste

Bring a large pot of water to a boil over high heat. Add the salt and potatoes and cook until tender, 10 to 15 minutes. Drain potatoes in a colander.

In a small skillet, heat the olive oil over medium heat. Add the garlic and sauté until tender, being careful not to brown it. Set aside.

Place a food mill over the empty pot in which the potatoes were cooked. Pass the potatoes through the mill, in batches, until all have been processed. Mix in the garlic mixture, chipotle purée, milk, and butter and stir until all the ingredients are incorporated. Season with salt and pepper to taste and serve immediately.

Chipotle Mashed Potato Cakes

Serves 4

2 cups leftover chipotle mashed potatoes (see above)

1 tablespoon olive oil

Form the cooled mashed potatoes into eight 2-inch patties. In a large nonstick skillet, heat the olive oil over medium-low heat. Cook the potato cakes until golden, about 5 minutes per side.

Southwestern Corn Pudding

Serves 8

Families from New England to the Deep South to the Southwest enjoy a version of corn pudding. Native Americans also prepare it, including the Pueblo Indians, and probably showed European settlers how to make it in the first place.

Green Chile Corn Bread

1 cup yellow cornmeal

1 cup all-purpose flour

¼ cup sugar

1 teaspoon baking soda

1 teaspoon salt

2 teaspoons baking powder

1 cup grated extra-sharp Cheddar cheese (about 4 ounces)

1 cup buttermilk

2 large eggs

4 tablespoons unsalted butter, melted and cooled

2 long green (Anaheim) chiles, roasted, peeled, seeded, and diced

1½ cups corn kernels

1 cup diced red bell pepper

1 long green (Anaheim) chile, stemmed, seeded, and diced

½ cup chopped green onions, white and light green parts

1 cup cotija cheese, crumbled, or queso fresco or Monterey jack

1 cup grated Monterey jack cheese

1 cup Red Sauce (see page 197)

2 cups buttermilk

4 eggs, slightly beaten

For the bread: Preheat an oven to 400°. Butter a 12 x 4-inch loaf pan, an 8-inch square pan, or a 9 x 5-inch loaf pan. In a large bowl, whisk together the cornmeal, flour, sugar, baking soda, salt, baking powder, and cheese. In a bowl, whisk together the buttermilk, eggs, and butter. Add the liquid mixture to the cornmeal mixture, stirring until just combined; stir in the green chiles. Spoon into the prepared loaf pan and bake until a tester inserted into the center comes out clean, 35 to 40 minutes. Let cool slightly, remove from the pan, and let cool completely.

Butter an 11 x 7-inch baking pan. Cut or break the cooled bread into 1-inch pieces. In a large bowl, mix together the bread cubes, corn, red pepper, chile, green onions, and the cheeses. Transfer to the prepared baking pan. In a bowl, whisk together the Red Sauce, buttermilk, and eggs. Pour over the bread mixture, cover with plastic wrap, and refrigerate for at least one hour or overnight.

Preheat an oven to 350°. Bake the pudding for 40 to 45 minutes and serve immediately.

Black Beans with Chipotle

Serves 8 to 10

The resurgence of long-lost heirloom beans in a rainbow of colors and patterns gives Southwesterners many options when it comes to bean cuisine. But the meaty goodness of black beans will always be a favorite on the Southwestern table. If you're serving just the family, you can easily cut this recipe in half. Leftovers are always a plus, though, especially for Black Bean Cakes (see page 133). Canned chipotle chiles in adobo sauce are readily available throughout the Southwest and in Latino markets elsewhere.

1 pound dried black beans, rinsed and picked over

12 cups water

6 cloves garlic, crushed

2 chipotle chiles in adobo sauce, finely chopped

3 cups finely chopped white onion (about 2 pounds)

1 teaspoon salt

2 tablespoons vegetable oil

2 long green (Anaheim) chiles, stemmed, seeded, and chopped

2 tablespoons finely chopped garlic

2 teaspoons dried oregano

2 teaspoons cumin seed, toasted and ground, or 1½ teaspoons ground cumin

Salt and freshly ground black pepper to taste

2 cups chicken stock

1 tablespoon freshly squeezed lime juice

½ cup chopped cilantro

½ cup crumbled cotija cheese (about 4 ounces) or grated Monterey jack or queso fresco, for garnish

Place the beans, water, cloves garlic, chipotle chiles, 2 cups of the onions, and salt in a large pot or Dutch oven and bring to a boil over high heat. Reduce the heat to low and simmer until the beans are tender, about 2 hours, adding more water if necessary.

In a sauté pan, heat the vegetable oil over medium heat. Add the remaining 1 cup onion, green chiles, chopped garlic, oregano, cumin, salt, and pepper. Cook until the onion is translucent and the vegetables are tender, 7 to 10 minutes.

When the beans are finished cooking, drain and return to the large pot or Dutch oven. Add the chicken stock and the sautéed vegetables. Over medium heat, simmer until the stock is absorbed and the beans are softened, about 30 minutes. Stir in the lime juice and cilantro; adjust the seasoning to taste.

Ladle a generous portion onto each bowl or plate. Sprinkle with cheese and serve immediately.

Green Chile Pilaf

Serves 6

Instead of the usual herbs, this verdant chile pilaf goes green with a uniquely Southwestern palette and pantry—tomatillos, jalapeño and poblano chiles, and pungent cilantro.

¼ pound tomatillos, husked, washed, and cut into quarters

1 jalapeño chile, seeded and chopped

1 cup water

¼ cup coarsely chopped onion

½ cup loosely packed cilantro leaves

1 teaspoon salt

1 poblano chile, roasted, peeled, and seeded

2 green onions, white and light green parts, trimmed and coarsely chopped

2 cloves garlic, peeled

1 tablespoon olive oil

1 cup rice, rinsed

Place the tomatillos, jalapeño, and water in a blender or a food processor. Mix just until chunky; then add the onion, cilantro, salt, poblano, green onions, and garlic. Purée until smooth, about 2 more minutes.

In a large, heavy saucepan, heat the olive oil over medium heat. Sauté the rice, stirring constantly, until golden and crackling, about 5 minutes. Pour in the purée and stir to combine. Cover and simmer until the liquid is absorbed and the rice is tender, 40 to 45 minutes. Stir with a fork and serve hot.

The heat of any chile dish can be controlled by the amount of chiles that you use. Did you know you can take a chile's "temperature"? Open up the chile and run your finger along a vein. Take a taste to check the heat and adjust the recipe accordingly.

Chapter 6

Breads and Tortillas

From Santa Fe to San Antonio, a basket of fresh, hot tortillas—"little cakes" in Spanish—is the daily bread on every table. We savor them plain or slathered with butter or honey. They're a scoop for a thick chili, a sop for a spicy stew, an edible "plate" for a hasty meal. Fried as wedges into crispy chips, they're the ultimate Southwestern snack.

It's a taste shaped by millennia of tradition: The Aztecs first made and ate corn tortillas (which they called *tlaxcalli*) more than 10,000 years ago. Mexican and Hispanic cooks have been patting them out ever since to use in countless ways. Ask anywhere in the Southwest how to make tostadas, burritos, nachos, enchiladas, fajitas, tacos, or quesadillas, and "Take a tortilla . . ." is the common reply.

Tortillas give a decidedly Southwestern spin to "you are what you eat." Those in the know can read them like a culinary road map: If they're slate-blue, they're New Mexican, made from the state's famed blue corn. In Arizona, flour tortillas—and the fillings they enclose—expand to mind-boggling dimension. While in Texas, "big" is the norm except for tortillas: Tex-Mex favorites like nachos and enchiladas use corn tortillas of modest size, about the diameter of a salad plate.

Tiny groceries to megasupermarkets feed the regional appetite with a plentiful supply of packaged tortillas. In cities and towns of any size, locals seek out neighborhood factories—tortillerias—for bags of these warm, soft flatbreads fresh off the fire. On busy Saturdays, even the smallest shop might crank out tortillas by the hundreds of dozens to satisfy customer demand.

Home cooks with a yen to make tortillas can do so here with ease, as the fixings are as common in the market down the street as butter or milk. While tortilla lovers in Iowa might find masa harina (a flour made from lime-slaked corn kernels to reconstitute with water) to make their dough, Southwestern shoppers tote home bags of moist corn masa, premixed to just the right consistency and ready to flatten into perfect rounds—with their own cast-iron tortilla press, of course!

Tortillas are hot, no doubt. But not just in the Southwest. Tortillas have gone mainstream, thanks to a national passion for Southwestern foods and flavors. Also turning up the heat is the current craze for fast-food wraps, whose global flavors transcend regional tags. In fact, tortillas have rolled into the number one spot as America's most popular ethnic bread.

Credit, too, for this tortilla mania must go to superstar Southwestern chefs like Vincent Guerithault of Phoenix. Filter tradition through a modern lens, and you have Vincent's Southwest Omelet (see page 119), Seared Tuna Tortilla Sandwich (see page 116), or Banana and Raspberry Tarts (see page 166).

Nothing tastes better than tortillas made by hand. This chapter tells you how to make basic corn, flour, and whole-wheat tortillas with ease. And as more than tortillas fill our bread basket, you'll also find recipes for delicious breads, muffins, and pancakes with a lively Southwestern twist.

Corn Tortillas

Makes 18 tortillas, 6 inches in diameter

Tortillas are the bread of the Southwest. We eat them daily, but even here, where you can buy them packaged in any grocery store, tortillas taste so much better when made by hand. They're very simple to prepare from only three ingredients: water, salt, and masa harina—ground lime-soaked dried corn—available in most supermarkets in the baking section. Masa harina is also sold in Latino groceries, a source, along with well-stocked cookware stores, for a comal (the traditional tortilla griddle) and cast-iron tortilla press.

2 cups masa harina
1½ cups water
½ teaspoon salt

Do Ahead { The cooled tortillas will keep, wrapped well in plastic wrap, in the refrigerator for up to 1 week.

Combine the masa harina, water, and salt in a large mixing bowl and stir until smooth. The dough should be slightly sticky and form a ball when pressed together. Divide the dough into 18 pieces the size of golf balls. Cover with a damp towel.

Heat a dry cast-iron skillet, nonstick pan, or comal until very hot. Line a tortilla press with 2 sheets of plastic wrap. Flatten each ball of dough in the tortilla press, then remove the plastic from the top and peel off the bottom sheet. Or, put a ball of dough between 2 sheets of plastic wrap or waxed paper and roll out into a circle about 6 inches in diameter. Lay the tortillas, one at a time, on the skillet and cook about 30 to 45 seconds per side, pressing the top of each tortilla with a spatula to make it puff.

Transfer the cooked tortillas to a clean kitchen towel. Stack the tortillas and wrap with the towel to keep them warm. Serve immediately.

Don't squeeze the tortilla press too hard, or the dough gets too thin to remove easily from the disk. Be sure the skillet or comal is hot or the tortilla will stick. Flip the tortilla when brown speckles develop on the bottom and the top bubbles. To fry tortilla chips, first test the temperature of the oil: Drop in one chip; if the chip bubbles to the surface, the oil is ready.

Flour Tortillas

With the invention of the wrap meal, flour tortillas are gaining new status. You'll find them small to oversize in most supermarkets, with stacks tinted spinach-green and tomato-red sharing shelf space with plain white ones. Traditionalists will enjoy this basic recipe just as it is. When you want to wrap and roll, mix in tasty extras like flecks of citrus zest or chopped herbs.

4 cups unbleached all-purpose flour
1½ teaspoons salt
4 teaspoons baking powder
3 tablespoons vegetable shortening or lard
1 to 1½ cups warm water

Do Ahead { The cooled tortillas will keep, wrapped well in plastic wrap, in the refrigerator for up to 3 days.

Stir together the flour, salt, and baking powder in a large bowl. With a fork, a pastry blender, or your fingertips, work the lard into the flour mixture until it is all incorporated. Add enough warm water to make a soft, not sticky, dough. Too much water makes tortillas tough, so add slowly.

Turn out onto a floured board and knead for 5 minutes. Cover with a clean towel or plastic wrap and allow to rest at least 30 minutes or up to 2 hours.

Divide the dough into balls of about ¼ cup each; flatten slightly. Cover with plastic wrap and let rest for 10 minutes.

Roll out the flattened balls with a rolling pin (not tapered), rolling from the center and turning a quarter turn after each roll, until the tortilla is about 8 or 9 inches in diameter. If the dough starts to shrink back to the center, allow it to rest for a few minutes before rolling again. Stack the tortillas between sheets of plastic wrap while waiting to cook them.

Over high heat, place a dry cast-iron skillet, nonstick pan, or comal. When the skillet is very hot (water sprinkled on it should dance across the surface), add a tortilla, being careful not to stretch it. When the bottom of the tortilla starts to show brown spots, about 30 seconds, turn over and cook another 15 to 30 seconds. Tortillas will get stiff if cooked too long, so cook them as quickly as possible, using higher and higher heat if necessary.

Transfer the cooked tortillas to a clean kitchen towel. Stack the tortillas and wrap the towel around them to keep them warm. Serve immediately.

 Work on a lightly floured surface, and keep flipping the tortilla as you roll it out, so both sides get redusted with flour. The flour keeps the dough from sticking to the work surface and the rolling pin.

Tortilla Chips

Makes 12 dozen chips

18 cooked tortillas
 4 cups peanut oil
Salt to taste

Do Ahead { The cooled tortilla chips will keep in an airtight container for up to 3 days.

Cut each tortilla into 8 triangular wedges (in half, in quarters, then in eighths). Place the oil in a heavy skillet or saucepan and heat to 375° over medium-high heat. Add the tortilla wedges, in batches, and cook until golden brown and crisp, 1 to 2 minutes. Remove with a slotted spoon and drain on paper towels. Season with salt to taste. Repeat with the remaining tortillas. Serve immediately.

Whole~Wheat Tortillas

Makes about 8 tortillas, 8 to 9 inches in diameter

Flour tortillas are relative newcomers: Wheat only arrived in the New World with the Spanish, while corn has grown here for millennia. In the Sonoran Desert, though, flour tortillas rule over corn, as wheat is the more popular crop. Whole-wheat tortillas have a pleasing brown color and pronounced flavor that complements most fillings.

1 cup all all-purpose flour
1 cup whole-wheat flour
2 teaspoons baking powder
1 teaspoon salt
2 tablespoons lard or vegetable shortening
½ to ¾ cup warm water

Do Ahead { To use the tortillas later on, wrap the hot tortillas in a dry towel until cool, put in plastic bags, seal, and refrigerate for up to 3 days. Refrigerated tortillas may get stiff, but they should soften again if put over a hot griddle for a few seconds on each side.

In a bowl, stir together the flours, baking powder, and salt. Blend in the lard or shortening with a fork, pastry blender, or your fingertips until the mixture is crumbly. Gradually stir in enough water, stirring just until the dough sticks together and forms a soft ball. (Too much water makes the tortillas tough, so add slowly.)

Turn the dough out onto a floured board and knead until smooth, about 5 minutes. Cover with a clean towel or plastic wrap and allow to rest at least 30 minutes or up to 2 hours.

Divide the dough into 8 portions and shape into balls; flatten slightly. Cover with plastic wrap and let rest for 10 minutes.

Roll out the flattened balls with a rolling pin (not tapered), rolling from the center and turning a quarter turn after each roll until the tortilla is about 9 inches in diameter. If the dough starts to shrink back to the center, allow it to rest for a few minutes before rolling again. Brush off any excess flour and trim rugged edges, if desired. Stack the tortillas between sheets of plastic wrap while waiting to cook them.

Over high heat, place a dry cast-iron skillet, nonstick pan, or comal. When the skillet is very hot (water sprinkled on it should dance across the surface), add a tortilla, being careful not to stretch it. When the bottom of the tortilla starts to show brown spots, about 30 seconds, turn it over and cook another 15 to 30 seconds. Tortillas will get stiff if cooked too long, so cook them as quickly as possible, using higher and higher heat if necessary.

Remove the tortilla from the griddle and transfer to a clean kitchen towel. Stack the tortillas and wrap with the towel around them to keep them warm. Serve immediately.

Blue Corn Bread

Roxsand Scocos

Makes 1 loaf

The Pueblo people of New Mexico prize blue corn for its distinctive color and subtle, earthy flavor. It is usually dried and ground into meal, which is actually a darkish gray. To achieve the sought-after lavender-blue color, it has to be treated with an alkaline substance such as culinary ashes or baking soda. In the Pueblo tradition, a paste of blue cornmeal and water is said to relieve aching joints. (Pictured page 155)

¾ cup blue cornmeal
½ teaspoon salt
3 teaspoons baking powder
⅓ cup sugar
1 cup all-purpose flour
1 egg, well beaten
1 cup whole milk
2 tablespoons bacon fat, melted
   and cooled slightly
1 cup corn kernels

Preheat an oven to 350°. Grease a 9 x 5-inch or 11 x 3-inch loaf pan.

Into a large bowl, sift together the cornmeal, salt, baking powder, sugar, and flour. In another bowl, whisk together the egg, milk, and bacon fat. Add the wet ingredients to the dry; fold in the corn kernels. Scrape into the prepared pan and bake until a tester inserted in the center comes out clean, about 35 to 40 minutes. Remove from the oven and let cool on a rack. When completely cool, turn the bread out onto a cutting board or platter, slice, and serve.

Dutch Oven Green Chile Corn Bread

Chuck Wiley

Chuck likes to bake this flavorful corn bread in a Dutch oven over a campfire. The cast-iron pan makes it especially crispy. You can also bake it at home in an uncovered pan, but it doesn't have the same sense of rustic, outdoor cooking. (Pictured right, with Blue Corn Bread, recipe page 153)

1 cup unsalted butter

¾ cup sugar

4 eggs

½ cup roasted, seeded, and diced green chiles (canned may be used)

1½ cups cream-style corn

½ cup grated Monterey jack cheese (may use jalapeño jack for more spark)

1 cup all-purpose flour

1 cup yellow cornmeal

2 tablespoons baking powder

1 teaspoon salt

Preheat an oven to 325°, light 18 charcoal briquettes, or use the glowing embers from a wood fire. Butter a 10-inch Dutch oven with a lid or a 9-inch square baking pan.

In a large bowl, beat together the butter and the sugar. Add the eggs, one at a time, beating well after each addition. Add the chiles, corn, and cheese and mix well. Sift together the flour, cornmeal, baking powder, and salt; add to the egg mixture and mix until smooth.

To make corn bread in the Dutch oven: Pour batter into the prepared Dutch oven. If baking over a fire, place the Dutch oven on top of 9 of the briquettes (or glowing embers) and place the remaining 9 briquettes (or glowing embers) on top of the lid. Briquettes cannot be touching the bottom of the Dutch oven. The legs of the Dutch oven should keep it elevated ½ inch or so above the briquettes. Ideally, the Dutch oven should be placed in a pit just deep and wide enough to hold it so it's surrounded by a consistent, even heat. Bake approximately 1 hour. If using an oven, bake until a tester inserted into the center comes out clean, about 1 hour.

To make corn bread in the baking pan: Pour batter into the prepared pan and bake in the preheated oven until a tester inserted into the center comes out clean, about 1 hour.

Don't feel compelled to remove every last bit of skin from the chiles after they've been roasted. In particular, don't rinse off the skin under water. You'll wash away the flavor that the roasting just put in.

Pumpkin~Pepita Bread

Makes 1 loaf

Instead of the usual nuts, this fragrant pumpkin bread mixes in pepitas—pumpkin seeds—for some crunch. Serve this slightly sweet quick bread with soup or salad for dinner, or as a breakfast treat. It stays moist for several days and freezes well, so it's a great food gift for the holidays. You can buy pepitas where Mexican ingredients are sold.

½ cup raw, unsalted pepitas
   (pumpkin seeds)
½ cup vegetable oil
2 eggs, lightly beaten
1 cup solid-pack pumpkin purée
⅓ cup water
2 cups all-purpose flour
1½ cups sugar
1 teaspoon baking soda
1 teaspoon ground cinnamon
½ teaspoon freshly grated
   nutmeg
½ teaspoon ground ginger
½ teaspoon ground allspice
½ teaspoon salt

Do Ahead { This moist bread will keep, wrapped in plastic wrap, for up to 3 days or can be frozen for up to 1 month.

Preheat an oven to 350°. Butter a 9 x 5-inch loaf pan.

In a small, dry skillet over medium heat, toast the pepitas until they pop and are lightly browned. With a chef's knife, coarsely chop them and set aside.

In a bowl, mix together the oil, eggs, pumpkin purée, and water. In a large bowl, mix together the remaining ingredients. Add the pumpkin mixture to the dry ingredients and stir until combined. Fold in the toasted, chopped pepitas and spoon the mixture into the prepared pan. Bake until a tester inserted into the center comes out clean, about 1 hour. Let cool and remove from the pan.

Corn Bread–Pecan Stuffing

Serves 8 to 10

With so many flavorful ingredients in this recipe, using a corn bread mix won't be a compromise but a sensible timesaver. If using canned stock, do not add salt until everything has been combined; then adjust salt to taste.

12 ounces chorizo
1 red bell pepper, seeded and
   diced (about 2 cups)
1 long green chile, seeded and
   diced (about ½ cup)
1½ cups diced white onion
6 cups crumbled corn bread
½ teaspoon dried oregano
1 tablespoon finely chopped
   parsley

Preheat an oven to 375°. Lightly butter an 11 x 7-inch pan.

In a large skillet over medium heat, cook the chorizo until browned, breaking it up as it cooks, about 10 minutes. Add the red bell pepper, chile, and onion and sauté until the vegetables are tender, about 5 minutes.

Place the corn bread in a large bowl. Add the oregano, parsley, pecans, and chorizo mixture. Stir in the butter and enough chicken

¾ cup toasted chopped pecans
6 tablespoons unsalted butter, melted
1 to 1¼ cups chicken stock
Salt and freshly ground black pepper to taste

stock to moisten the bread well. Spoon the stuffing into the prepared pan, cover with aluminum foil, and bake until heated through, about 30 minutes.

 Bake the casserole uncovered if you prefer a crusty stuffing.

Chipotle Cheese Bread

Makes 2 loaves

Jalapeños are probably the most popular chile in the Southwest. This bread contains both the fresh and the dried, smoked version called chipotles. The cheese counteracts some of the heat from the chiles and adds great flavor.

Spread with Achiote Butter (see page 91) and serve with your favorite soup or salad. It's also a great sandwich bread, stuffed with smoked turkey, Chipotle Mayonnaise (see page 204), Monterey jack cheese, avocado, tomatoes, and sprouts.

1 package active dry yeast
¼ cup plus 1 teaspoon sugar
2 cups warm water (100° to 110°)
5 to 6 cups unbleached all-purpose flour
2 teaspoons salt
1 teaspoon ground cinnamon
2 jalapeño chiles, finely diced
1 cup grated Monterey jack cheese
2 chipotle chiles in adobo sauce, puréed and strained

In a bowl, stir together the yeast, 1 teaspoon of the sugar, and the water. Allow to sit for 5 minutes until the yeast is foamy.

In the bowl of an electric mixer or in a large bowl, stir together 5 cups of the flour, the remaining ¼ cup sugar, salt, and cinnamon; add the jalapeños and the cheese. Add the yeast-water mixture and the chipotle purée and mix well, either by hand or with the dough hook of the mixer. The dough should be soft; add more flour if necessary. If kneading by hand, turn the dough out onto a floured board and knead until the dough is smooth and elastic, about 10 minutes. If kneading in the mixer, knead until the dough pulls away from the side of the bowl and is smooth and elastic, about 5 minutes. Place the dough in a large, lightly oiled bowl, cover with a clean kitchen towel or plastic wrap, and set aside to rise in a warm place. Let rise until doubled, about 1 hour.

Punch the dough down and, with floured hands, shape into two oblong loaves. Place the loaves on a parchment paper-lined baking sheet and place in a warm place to rise. Let rise until doubled, 45 minutes to 1 hour.

Preheat an oven to 400°. With a sharp knife, cut ½-inch deep slashes about 2 inches apart along the length of the loaves. Place a baking sheet in the center of the hot oven and bake until the loaves are lightly browned and sound hollow when tapped, 25 to 30 minutes. Remove from the oven and transfer the loaves to a cooling rack.

Banana~Pecan Pancakes with Pecan Syrup

Serves 6

If you see a pecan and just think "Georgia," reset your sights a little further west. Texas is the largest producer of native pecans and second only to Georgia in production of hybrid (orchard) nuts. In fact, since 1919, the pecan has been the state tree of Texas. These melt-in-your-mouth, crunchy pancakes are elegant enough for brunch, but just as good at a camp-out.

Syrup

2 cups granulated sugar
1 cup boiling water
⅔ cup toasted pecans

Pancakes

1½ cups all-purpose flour
1 teaspoon baking powder
1 teaspoon baking soda
¼ teaspoon salt
1 tablespoon brown sugar
1 cup buttermilk
¼ cup milk
1 egg
1 tablespoon unsalted butter, melted
1 teaspoon pure vanilla extract
⅔ cup toasted pecans
1½ cups thinly sliced ripe bananas (about 2)
2 to 3 tablespoons unsalted butter

Do Ahead { The syrup can be made up to 1 week ahead, covered, and refrigerated.

For the syrup: Place the granulated sugar in a heavy saucepan. Over low heat, melt the sugar, stirring constantly with a wooden spoon until the sugar becomes a clear brown liquid. Remove from the heat and add the boiling water carefully so it doesn't spatter. Return to low heat and stir until the syrup is smooth and all the sugar is dissolved. Stir in the pecans and cool.

For the pancakes: Sift together the flour, baking powder, baking soda, salt, and brown sugar. Set aside. In a bowl, whisk together the buttermilk, milk, egg, melted butter, and vanilla. Add to the dry ingredients and stir until just combined. Fold in the pecans and bananas.

In a large nonstick skillet over medium heat, melt 1 tablespoon of the butter. Ladle the mixture into the pan in ¼-cup measures. When bubbles appear (about 2 minutes), flip the pancakes over and cook until golden brown, another 1 or 2 minutes. Remove the cooked pancakes and keep warm in a 250° oven. Repeat with the remaining batter, adding additional butter as needed.

To serve, place 2 pancakes on each plate and pass the pecan syrup.

Cranberry Cornmeal Muffins

Makes 14 to 16 (2½-inch) muffins

Mixing in cornmeal with the flour gives these Thanksgiving favorites a crunchy Southwestern texture. But as dried cranberries are now available all year, you don't have to wait until fall to make them. A basket of these muffins hot from the oven will wow a Sunday brunch.

1¼ cups all-purpose flour
¾ cup cornmeal
½ cup sugar
1 tablespoon baking powder
1 teaspoon baking soda
1 teaspoon ground cinnamon
¼ teaspoon salt
1 cup dried cranberries
1¼ cups buttermilk
¼ cup unsalted butter, melted
2 large eggs

Do Ahead { The muffins are best eaten the day they are made, but they can be frozen, well wrapped, for up to 1 month.

Preheat an oven to 425°. Spray standard 2½-inch muffins tins with nonstick cooking spray or line with muffin cup liners.

Combine the flour, cornmeal, sugar, baking powder, baking soda, cinnamon, and salt in a large bowl; mix well. Add the cranberries and stir to coat.

In a 2-cup measure, measure the buttermilk; add the butter and eggs and whisk together until all is blended. Add the liquid mixture to the dry one and fold in quickly and gently with a rubber spatula just until the dry ingredients are moistened. Spoon into the prepared muffin cups, filling each about three-fourths full.

Bake until the tops are golden and the edges are slightly browned, 15 to 20 minutes. Let cool in the pan for about 5 minutes; remove from the pan and serve warm.

Refrigerator Orange Rolls

Makes 2 dozen

Today, housing developments replace orange groves in the Valley of the Sun around Phoenix, but many homeowners there still have their own fruit-bearing trees. These rolls are a terrific way to showcase the juicy fruit. Because the dough keeps for days in the refrigerator, it's also great to have on hand during the holidays.

1 package active dry yeast
¼ cup warm water (110° to 115°)
¼ cup plus 1 teaspoon sugar
1 cup milk, at room temperature
3 tablespoons unsalted butter,
   at room temperature
1 teaspoon salt
2 eggs, beaten
3 to 3½ cups all-purpose flour

Filling

½ cup sugar
3 tablespoons grated orange
   zest

½ cup unsalted butter, melted

Do Ahead { The dough can be made up to 5 days ahead, covered, and refrigerated.

Stir together the yeast, warm water, and 1 teaspoon of the sugar in a small bowl and allow to sit until foamy, about 5 minutes.

In a large bowl, combine the milk, 3 tablespoons butter, remaining ¼ cup of the sugar and the salt; stir until the butter is melted and the sugar is dissolved. Add the yeast mixture, eggs, and 1½ cups of the flour. Beat until well mixed. Add enough of the remaining flour to make a stiff dough. Knead on a floured board until smooth and elastic, 5 to 10 minutes.

Place the dough in a lightly oiled bowl, cover with plastic wrap, and refrigerate overnight or up to 4 days.

For the filling: Combine the orange zest and sugar.

Assembly: Remove the dough from the refrigerator and allow to come to room temperature. Preheat an oven to 400°. Lightly butter 24 standard muffin cups (2½ inches in diameter).

Pull off a piece of the dough the size of a small egg. Dip the dough in melted butter, then in orange-sugar mixture. Stretch the dough into a 6- to 8-inch rope and tie into a knot. Place in a greased muffin cup. Repeat with the remaining dough. Bake for 12 to 15 minutes, or until lightly browned. Serve warm.

A change of filling makes these rolls altogether new: For the orange-sugar filling, try poppy, cumin, or sesame seeds instead.

Chapter 7

Desserts

Was the great Aztec king Montezuma the world's first chocaholic? He was said to imbibe fifty golden goblets of chocolate every day to boost his sexual prowess. For the Aztecs, chocolate was so exalted and so macho a beverage that only aristocracy and then only men were permitted to drink it. It's no wonder that this treasured confection is celebrated as one of Mexico's great culinary gifts to the American Southwest and to the rest of the world.

Though Montezuma relished chocolate as an elixir of the gods, it was bitter medicine to the Spanish explorers who tried it at his court. (In fact chocolate comes from an Aztec word that in part means "bitter water.") The liquid was not sweetened in any way, just flavored with chiles and perhaps vanilla. Despite their dislike for its taste, the Spanish found the beverage curiously energizing. So chocolate returned with them to Europe, where they "improved" it with sugar and cinnamon. It was an instant hit.

In sweet form, chocolate also became a popular beverage throughout the Spanish colonies, including the area that would become the Southwest. Mexican chocolate, part of the complex mixture of ingredients in the traditional Southwestern sauce known as a mole, is still spiced with cinnamon and sweetened with sugar in the Spanish style.

Montezuma and the Spanish conquistadors would all certainly approve of the scrumptious desserts that follow in this chapter. Donna Nordin, chef and owner of two Arizona branches of Cafe Terra Cotta, fashions a classic Southwestern fast food—the taco—in chocolate and fills it with a luscious hazelnut cream (see Chocolate Tacos Filled with Hazelnut-Chocolate Mousse, page 170). Chocolate and chiles, a favorite pairing of Southwestern chefs, find new interpretation in Stephan Pyles's devilish Chocolate Diablo Bread Pudding (page 176) and John Rivera Sedlar's Chocolate Tamales with Candied Chiles (page 175).

Here are also a multitude of nonchocolate desserts that take your taste buds in delightful directions (vanilla, after all, is another food legacy from ancient Mexico). Choose from tarts, pies, puddings, and cookies, all equally wonderful, and all with a uniquely Southwestern point of view.

Indian Pudding

Loretta Barrett Oden　　　　**Serves 6 to 8**

This intriguing Native American dessert is perfect for entertaining since it bakes for 2½ hours. It's amazing how all the milk gets absorbed, making the pudding creamy and the top slightly crusty. Loretta uses wild ginger—snakeroot—but it's not available in markets or by mail order. Use ground ginger instead.

5 tablespoons butter

⅔ cup cornmeal

½ teaspoon ground ginger (Native American equivalent is called snakeroot)

¼ teaspoon freshly grated nutmeg

4 cups whole milk

1 cup maple syrup

1½ cups dried cherries

Blackberry, cranberry, or apricot syrup, or honey-sweetened whipped cream, for accompaniment

Preheat an oven to 300°. Using 1 tablespoon of the butter, coat the bottom and sides of a 2-quart (8-inch-square) casserole dish.

In a small bowl, stir together the cornmeal, ginger, and nutmeg. Place 3 cups of the milk and the maple syrup in a saucepan over medium heat. Bring just to a boil, reduce the heat to low, and add the ¼ cup butter. Gradually whisk in the cornmeal mixture and cook until thickened, about 5 minutes. Fold in the dried cherries. Spoon the mixture into the prepared casserole; pour the remaining 1 cup milk over the top of the pudding. Do not stir.

Bake until the milk has been absorbed and the top of the pudding is golden brown, approximately 2½ hours. Serve warm with syrup or honey-sweetened whipped cream.

To make a delicious blackberry coulis, purée fresh or frozen blackberries in a blender with honey to taste. Then spoon the sauce into a squeeze bottle and drizzle over individual servings of pudding.

Banana and Raspberry Tarts

Vincent Guerithault

Until recently, flavoring ingredients were never added to tortillas; but now all kinds of savory tortillas can be purchased in grocery stores. Vincent takes it one step further and adds orange juice and zest to make this unique dessert. This recipe works equally well with sheets of frozen puff pastry.

Orange-Flavored Tortillas

1 cup unbleached all-purpose flour

¼ teaspoon salt

1 teaspoon baking powder

2 tablespoons unsalted butter

1 teaspoon grated orange zest

¼ cup freshly squeezed orange juice

1 to 2 tablespoons water

Filling

2 bananas, cut into ¼-inch slices

1 cup fresh raspberries

2 to 3 tablespoons confectioners' sugar, depending on the sweetness of the raspberries

½ cup freshly squeezed fresh orange juice

1 tablespoon sugar

2 tablespoons butter, cut into ¼-inch pieces

For the tortillas: In a large bowl, stir together the flour, salt, and baking powder. With a pastry blender, a fork, or your fingertips, work in the butter and orange zest until incorporated. Gradually add the orange juice and enough water to make a soft, not sticky, dough. Turn out onto a floured board and knead until smooth, about 5 minutes. Cover with a clean towel or plastic wrap and allow to rest for 30 minutes. Divide the dough into balls, about ¼ cup each; flatten slightly. Cover with plastic wrap and let rest for 10 minutes. Roll out each ball between sheets of waxed paper into a flat round about 8 inches in diameter. Heat a heavy skillet over high heat; when very hot, add a tortilla and cook until small brown dots appear on the underside, about 1 minute. Turn over and cook the other side, about 30 seconds more. Remove, and repeat with the remaining tortillas.

For the filling: In a bowl, mix together the bananas, raspberries, confectioners' sugar, and orange juice. Marinate for 15 minutes. Strain the fruit over a small saucepan, reserving the accumulated juice in the pan.

Preheat an oven to 375°.

Assembly: Sprinkle the granulated sugar evenly on top of the cooked tortillas. Place the tortillas on a baking sheet. Arrange the strained fruit on the tortillas, stopping one inch from the edge, and top the fruit with bits of butter. Bake the tarts until lightly browned and crisp, about 15 minutes.

Heat the pan with reserved juices over medium-high heat; bring to a boil, reduce the heat, and simmer until the mixture is thick enough to use as a glaze, about 10 minutes. Remove the tarts from the oven and spread the thickened juices over the tops of the tarts and serve.

The tortillas can also be flavored with lime, lemon, or grapefruit.

Prickly Pear Sorbet

In the Southwest we can pick prickly pear fruit—called tunas—right off the cactus nine months of the year. Many grocery stores, specialty stores, and Latino markets also sell them. It's also possible to buy prickly pear purée (see Mail-Order Sources, page 217) and prickly pear syrup. The syrup is too sweet to use in this recipe, however. The inedible skins of the fruit are green or light purple, and the ripe pulp is a brilliant magenta that makes a beautiful sorbet.

1 cup sugar
½ cup water
2 cups prickly pear fruit (tunas), peeled
1 tablespoon raspberry liqueur (Chambord or framboise)
Raspberries and lime slices, for garnish

Combine the sugar and water in a small saucepan over medium-high heat. Bring to a boil, reduce the heat and simmer until the sugar is dissolved, about 2 minutes. Let cool completely.

Purée the prickly pears in a blender or food processor; strain into a bowl. Add the cooled sugar syrup and raspberry liqueur. Refrigerate until well chilled.

Pour the mixture into an ice cream machine. Process according to the manufacturer's directions. Serve in margarita glasses with fresh raspberries and a slice of lime.

 Even more than raspberries, prickly pear fruit is plagued by tiny seeds. To remove them, the fruit is puréed, then strained. To keep the strainer from getting clogged, spoon the purée into the strainer and first shake some liquid through. Then force through the remaining purée with a rubber spatula or the bowl of a ladle.

Caliente Chocolate Ice Cream

Makes about 4 cups

This is ice cream with a buzz. You don't really taste the chile, but you feel a little burn just after you swallow. It's a great sensation. If you want even more heat in the ice cream, leave the seeds in the serrano chile while it steeps in the milk mixture, then strain them out.

1½ cups milk

1½ cups heavy cream

1 vanilla bean

1 cup Dutch-process unsweetened cocoa powder

1 serrano chile, stemmed,
seeded, and coarsely chopped

5 egg yolks

¾ cup sugar

⅛ teaspoon salt

Place the milk and cream in a saucepan. Cut the vanilla bean in half horizontally and scrape the soft interior into the pan, along with the cut bean. Add the cocoa powder and chile. Bring the mixture to a boil over medium-high heat, whisking until well blended. Remove the pan from the heat and allow the mixture to steep, covered, for at least 30 minutes or up to 1 hour.

In a large bowl with an electric mixer, whisk together the yolks, sugar, and salt. Strain the milk mixture into the egg mixture and whisk until well combined. Pour the mixture back into the saucepan and cook over medium heat, stirring constantly, until it coats the back of a spoon and reaches a temperature of 170°, 5 to 10 minutes. Strain into a clean bowl set over a bowl of ice; let cool. When cold, transfer the mixture to an ice cream maker and freeze according to the manufacturer's directions.

Chocolate Tacos Filled with Hazelnut~ Chocolate Mousse

Donna Nordin

That Donna Nordin is a chocolate artist as well as a fine cook is amply demonstrated with this whimsical dessert. The tacos are easily formed out of rounds of melted chocolate draped over dowels until they harden. The shells make an eye-catching presentation, even simply filled with a flavored whipped cream or soft ice cream.

Mousse

8 ounces bittersweet chocolate, coarsely chopped

½ cup heavy cream

3 tablespoons confectioners' sugar

2 tablespoons hazelnut liqueur (Frangelico)

½ cup toasted, ground hazelnuts

Chocolate Tacos

1 pound bittersweet chocolate, coarsely chopped

¼ cup toasted, coarsely chopped hazelnuts

Raspberry Sauce

1 cup frozen raspberries, thawed

1 cup seedless raspberry jam

Papaya-Kiwi Salsa

1 papaya, peeled, seeded, and finely diced

3 kiwis, peeled and finely diced

1 tablespoon confectioners' sugar

Do Ahead The raspberry sauce and chocolate taco shells can be made a day ahead and refrigerated. The salsa can be made up to 4 hours before serving. The mousse can be made a day ahead and refrigerated but needs to come to room temperature to pipe into the taco shells.

For the mousse: Place the chocolate in the top of a double boiler over hot, not boiling, water. Melt completely, stirring occasionally, about 5 minutes. Place the cream in a bowl and, with a whisk or electric mixer, whip until soft peaks form. Add the sugar and liqueur and whisk until completely incorporated (do not overbeat or it will be difficult to fold in the chocolate). Fold in the nuts. Remove the chocolate from the heat and gently fold into the whipped cream. Refrigerate the mousse until firm enough to pipe, about 1 hour or up to 1 day ahead.

For the tacos: On parchment paper draw 12 rounds, each 4½ inches in diameter. Cut out the rounds with scissors and arrange them on a work surface. Place the chocolate in the top of a double boiler over hot, not boiling, water. Melt completely, stirring occasionally, about 10 minutes. Remove from the heat. Using the back of a spoon, spread a thin layer of chocolate smoothly over each circle. Sprinkle half of each circle with 1 teaspoon of chopped hazelnuts. Let sit until the chocolate begins to set but is still pliable, about 30 minutes. Drape the pliable parchment-chocolate discs over 2 wooden dowels, 1 inch thick and 20 inches long, and balance over a roasting pan. Place the roasting pan in the refrigerator and chill the tacos until hard. Remove the tacos from the dowels and carefully peel off the parchment paper.

For the raspberry sauce: In a food processor or blender, purée the raspberries; strain into a bowl. Stir in the jam and mix well. Refrigerate, covered, until ready to serve.

For the papaya-kiwi salsa: Mix all the ingredients in a bowl. Let the flavors marry for at least 30 minutes. Refrigerate, covered, until ready to serve.

Assembly: Place the mousse in a pastry bag fitted with a star tip. If the mousse has been chilled until it's too firm to pipe, let it come to room temperature and then fill the pastry bag. Pipe the mousse into the chocolate taco shells. Refrigerate until ready to serve. Place about 1 tablespoon of raspberry sauce on the bottom of each of 12 plates; top with a mousse-filled taco. Spoon a tablespoon of papaya-kiwi salsa on the side of the taco. Serve immediately.

 Even a bit of moisture in melted chocolate will make it seize into an unusable mess. To prevent such a disaster, wipe off any moisture from the bottom of the double boiler after the chocolate melts.

Dark Chocolate–Jalapeño Ice Cream Sundae

Janos Wilder

Serves 10 to 12

"Chocolate truffle meets jalapeño chile" is an apt description of this addictive frozen confection, which delivers double the chocolate as the sauce is chocolate, too. Note that the eggs in this recipe do not get cooked, so if you are concerned about salmonella, be sure of your egg source—or substitute Caliente Chocolate Ice Cream (see page 169).

Dark Chocolate–Jalapeño Ice Cream

3 cups half-and-half

1 jalapeño chile, stemmed, seeded, and julienned

10 ounces bittersweet chocolate, finely chopped

3 eggs

¾ cup sugar

1 cup heavy cream

½ cup pecans, toasted

White Chocolate Sauce

½ cup heavy cream

8 ounces white chocolate, finely chopped

Candied Pecans

1½ cups water

1½ cups plus ⅓ cup sugar

1½ cups pecan pieces

Do Ahead { The white chocolate sauce can be made up to 3 days ahead, covered, and refrigerated. Rewarm the sauce in a double boiler before serving. The candied pecans can be made up to 1 week ahead.

For the ice cream: In a saucepan over medium-high heat, bring the half-and-half and jalapeño to a boil. Remove from the heat and add the chocolate. Let sit for 1 or 2 minutes and then stir until the chocolate is melted and incorporated into the half-and-half. Let cool and refrigerate overnight.

Strain the half-and-half mixture and discard the jalapeño. In a large bowl with an electric mixer, beat the eggs and sugar at medium speed until fluffy and light in color. Turn the mixer to low and mix in the chocolate mixture, cream, and pecans. Transfer to an ice cream freezer and freeze according to the manufacturer's directions.

For the white chocolate sauce: In a small pan over medium heat, bring the cream to a boil. Remove from the heat and add the white chocolate. Allow to sit 1 or 2 minutes and then stir until the chocolate is completely melted.

For the candied pecans: In a saucepan over high heat, combine the water and 1½ cups of the sugar and bring to a boil; boil for 2 minutes, or until the sugar is dissolved. Add the pecan pieces and boil for 2 minutes more. Drain the pecans well. Place the remaining ⅓ cup sugar in a bowl and add the warm pecans. Toss well, coating evenly, and spread them on a baking sheet lined with parchment paper. Allow to dry about 2 hours; use immediately or store in an airtight container for up to a week.

Assembly: Place 2 scoops of ice cream in each bowl. Drizzle with the white chocolate sauce and sprinkle candied pecans on top.

Mexican Chocolate Profiteroles

Serves 8

Primarily used for a beverage, Mexican chocolate already has sugar and cinnamon added to it. This Southwestern confection gives a classic French dessert a regional accent.

Cinnamon Ice Cream

1½ cups milk
1½ cups heavy cream
1 vanilla bean
2 cinnamon sticks
5 egg yolks
¾ cup sugar
⅛ teaspoon salt

Mexican Chocolate Sauce

½ cup water
½ cup sugar
1 cinnamon stick
⅓ cup unsweetened Dutch-process cocoa powder
2 tablespoons unsalted butter, at room temperature

Profiteroles

1 cup all-purpose flour
2 tablespoons unsweetened Dutch-process cocoa powder
½ teaspoon ground cinnamon
1 tablespoon sugar
⅛ teaspoon salt
1 cup water
6 tablespoons unsalted butter
4 eggs

For the ice cream: Place the milk and cream in a saucepan. With a sharp knife, slice the vanilla bean in half lengthwise, scrape the soft interior into the milk, then add the split bean and the cinnamon sticks. Bring the mixture to a boil over medium-high heat; remove the pan from the heat and let the mixture steep, covered, for at least an hour. With an electric mixer, whisk together the yolks, sugar, and salt. Add the milk mixture in a stream and beat until combined. Pour the custard back into the saucepan and cook over medium heat, stirring constantly, until it coats the back of a spoon and reaches a temperature of 170°, 5 to 10 minutes. Strain and let cool. Freeze in an ice cream maker according to the manufacturer's directions.

For the chocolate sauce: Place the water, sugar, and cinnamon sticks in a heavy saucepan over medium heat and bring to a boil, stirring occasionally; cook until the sugar is dissolved, about 2 minutes. Remove the pan from the heat and allow to sit until the sugar syrup takes on the cinnamon flavor, about 2 hours. Remove the cinnamon stick and return the pan to medium heat. Bring the mixture to a boil and whisk in cocoa until the sauce is smooth. Reduce the heat to low and whisk in the butter. Refrigerate until ready to use.

For the profiteroles: Preheat an oven to 425°. Line 2 baking sheets with parchment paper. Sift together the flour, cocoa, cinnamon, sugar, and salt. Combine the water and butter in a heavy saucepan and bring to a boil. Remove from the heat. Add the flour mixture and beat with a wooden spoon until incorporated. Set the pan over medium heat and beat until the mixture pulls away from the sides of the pan. Let cool slightly and then beat in the eggs, one at a time. Continue beating until the dough is smooth. Spoon the dough into a pastry bag fitted with a large plain tip and pipe about twenty-four 2-inch circles onto the prepared baking sheets, or drop by rounded teaspoonful 2 inches apart onto cookie sheets. Bake until puffed and the tops begin to brown, 25 to 30 minutes. With a serrated knife, make a horizontal 1-inch slit in the side of each puff to allow steam to escape. Bake 2 more minutes. Let cool completely.

Assembly: Cut each puff along its slit so it opens like a book. Spoon ice cream into each puff and place 3 filled profiteroles onto each serving plate. Top with chocolate sauce and serve immediately.

Chocolate Tamales with Candied Chiles

John Rivera Sedlar   Serves 6

If you've sworn off anything candied thanks to fruitcake, this incredible dessert will make you eat your words—and you'll love every bite. It's an amazing chocolate tour de force from a master Southwestern chef. You can find decorative stencils at most cookware stores.

Tamales

10 ounces semi-sweet chocolate, finely chopped

1¾ cups heavy cream

½ cup finely chopped toasted pecans

12 large dried corn husks, soaked in warm water for at least 30 minutes

2 ounces white chocolate, finely chopped

Candied Chiles

1 cup sugar

½ cup freshly squeezed lemon juice

3 Anaheim chiles, seeded, deveined, and cut into ¼-inch dice (about 1½ cups)

½ cup cocoa powder

Do Ahead { The tamales can be made a day ahead and refrigerated. The candied chiles can be made up to 3 days ahead, covered, and refrigerated; keep them in the lemon-sugar mixture until ready to serve.

For the tamales: Place the chocolate in a large bowl. In a saucepan, bring the cream to a boil over medium-high heat. Remove from the heat and pour over the finely chopped chocolate; allow to stand 3 to 4 minutes. With a whisk or rubber spatula stir the cream-chocolate mixture until smooth, about 1 minute. Stir in the nuts. Refrigerate until the chocolate mixture is firm but pliable, 45 minutes to 1 hour. Do not let it harden completely.

Remove 6 of the corn husks from the warm water; clean and pat them dry with a paper towel. Lay the dried husks out on a work surface and divide the chocolate evenly among them, placing the chocolate in the center of the husks. Fold the sides of each corn husk over the chocolate into a rectangle. Refrigerate until firm, about 1 hour.

Remove the tamales from the refrigerator and unwrap the corn husks, placing the tamales on waxed paper. Melt the white chocolate in the top of a double boiler over hot, not boiling, water, or in a microwave for about 30 seconds on high power, stirring frequently. Dip a fork into the melted white chocolate and shake it back and forth over the tamales to make a decorative pattern. Return the tamales to the refrigerator until the white chocolate hardens.

For the candied chiles: Place the sugar and lemon juice in a small skillet over high heat and bring to a boil; reduce the heat and simmer until the sugar is dissolved, about 2 minutes. Add the chiles and remove from the heat; let cool. Remove and discard the excess liquid. Set the candied chiles aside. Continued page 176.

Assembly: Remove the remaining corn husks from the water, clean, and pat dry. Tear a ¼-inch strip from the edge of each corn husk and use it to tie the pointed end of the corn husk to form 6 corn husk containers. On 6 large white plates, place a decorative stencil on the left-hand side of the plate and, with a sieve, gently sprinkle the cocoa powder over the stencil. Lift the stencil. Place a tied corn husk on the right side of each plate and gently place a tamale in the center. Spoon some candied chiles over the bottom end of each tamale. Serve immediately.

Chocolate Diablo Bread Pudding

Stephan Pyles   Serves 8

Says Stephan: "Who would have thought—chiles for dessert? But you're really going to be surprised what a good combination chocolate and pasillas are." He serves this chocolate sensation with vanilla ice cream, which combats any heat from the chile. Be aware that the heat is quite subtle at first, but intensifies as the pudding sits.

3 pasilla chiles (substitute chile negro)
3 cups milk
6 ounces semisweet chocolate, chopped
5 eggs
1½ cups firmly packed brown sugar
1½ teaspoons ground cinnamon
2 tablespoons pure vanilla extract
¼ cup dried cherries
6 ounces French bread, cut into cubes
1 cup chopped walnuts
3 tablespoons unsalted butter, cut into ¼-inch pieces
Vanilla ice cream, for accompaniment

Soak the dried chiles in warm water until soft, about 30 minutes. Drain the chiles, then remove and discard the stem and seeds. Purée the chiles in a blender or mini food processor. Strain the purée into a small bowl (there should be about 3 tablespoons of chile purée).

Place the milk and chocolate in a saucepan and cook, stirring, until the chocolate is melted. Remove from the heat and reserve.

In a large mixing bowl, whisk together the eggs, sugar, cinnamon, vanilla, and pasilla purée. Slowly add the chocolate mixture and stir until thoroughly combined. Add the cherries and bread cubes; weight with a plate so the bread is fully submersed in the liquid. Allow to stand for at least 30 minutes or up to 1 hour.

Preheat an oven to 350°. Lightly butter a 10-inch round cake pan with 2-inch sides. Pour the bread pudding into the pan. Sprinkle the top with walnuts and dot with butter pieces. Bake until a toothpick inserted in the center comes out clean, about 50 minutes. Allow to cool slightly and serve warm with vanilla ice cream.

Walnuts taste better if you toast them in a dry skillet or in the oven (see page 216). But it's best to first boil them briefly to remove their bitter skin.

South~of~the~Border Chocolate Cookies

Makes about 60 cookies

These are addictive and easy to make, and the dough keeps in the refrigerator up to a day ahead, ready to bake and serve. If you want larger or smaller cookies, adjust the diameter of the dough cylinder, but also remember to adjust the cooking time. (Pictured page 181)

1¼ cups all-purpose flour

⅓ cup unsweetened Dutch-process cocoa powder

¼ teaspoon ancho chile powder or chile powder

¼ teaspoon salt

½ cup unsalted butter, softened

¾ cup sugar

1 large egg

2 tablespoons sugar mixed with 2 teaspoons ground cinnamon

Do Ahead { The cookies can be made up to 3 days ahead of time and stored in an airtight container or frozen, tightly wrapped, for up to 1 month.

Sift together the flour, cocoa, chile powder, and salt over a piece of waxed paper. Set aside.

With an electric mixer, beat the butter in a large bowl until creamy, about 1 minute. Add the sugar and beat until the mixture is light in color, 3 to 4 minutes more. Scrape down the sides of the bowl; beat in the egg. Gradually add the flour-cocoa mixture to the butter mixture and beat until well mixed.

Divide the dough in half and set each half on its own 18-inch-long piece of plastic wrap. Form both pieces of dough into cylinders approximately 1½ inches in diameter, using the plastic wrap as a guide. Wrap tightly and refrigerate until firm, at least 2 hours. Or, rolls can be frozen at this point for up to 2 weeks.

Preheat an oven to 350°. Using a sharp knife, slice each cylinder into ¼-inch slices; place the slices on ungreased baking sheets and bake until set, about 10 minutes. Remove the baking sheets from the oven and let the cookies cool a few minutes. Sprinkle the baked cookies with the cinnamon-sugar mixture. With a spatula, transfer them to a wire rack to cool completely.

Be sure to sprinkle on the cinnamon-sugar topping while the cookies are still hot or the mixture won't stick.

Chile Snaps

Makes 2 dozen 4-inch cookies

The hint of heat is so subtle in these sugar cookies that when it hits, it takes you by surprise. For the best flavor, be sure the chile powder that you use is the pure spice, without any additions or preservatives. Around here, we like to cut these cookies out with a cactus-shaped cookie cutter because the frosting is such a lively shade of cactus green. (Pictured page 181)

Cookies

- 2 cups all-purpose flour
- 2 teaspoons baking powder
- 1 teaspoon baking soda
- 1 teaspoon ground allspice
- 1 teaspoon ground cinnamon
- ½ teaspoon chile powder
- ¼ teaspoon salt
- ½ cup unsalted butter, at room temperature
- 1 cup sugar
- 1 egg

Frosting

- 2 ounces cream cheese
- 4 tablespoons unsalted butter
- 1 cup confectioners' sugar
- ¼ cup homemade Pepper Jelly (see page 33) or commercially prepared
- 1 or 2 drops green food coloring

Do Ahead { Store the frosted cookies in an airtight container for up to 1 week.

For the cookies: Sift together the flour, baking powder, baking soda, allspice, cinnamon, chile powder, and salt. Set aside.

In a large bowl with an electric mixer, beat the butter and sugar together at medium speed until the sugar is dissolved, about 2 minutes. Add the egg and mix again for 2 minutes. Reduce the speed to low and gradually add in the sifted flour mixture, beating until just incorporated. Spoon out the mixture onto plastic wrap, form into a disc, wrap well, and refrigerate for at least 2 hours or overnight.

Preheat an oven to 375°. Butter 2 baking sheets or line them with parchment paper. On a floured board, roll out the refrigerated dough ⅛ inch thick. Cut into Southwestern shapes with cookie cutters and place on the prepared cookie sheets. Bake until crisp and golden, 8 to 10 minutes. Let cool slightly and remove to a wire rack. Let cool completely.

For the frosting: In a bowl with an electric mixer, beat all ingredients until smooth. Spread thinly on the cooled cookies.

 A basket of these cookies in holiday shapes with a jar of homemade pepper jelly makes a terrific holiday gift.

Pistachio~Orange Wafers

Roxsand Scocos

Makes about 72 cookies

Some of the country's best pistachio nuts are cultivated in Arizona, and orange orchards also flourish in the central and southern parts of the state. Roxsand really shows off both Arizona crops in these delicious cookies. (Pictured, right, with South-of-the-Border Cookies, recipe page 178, and Chile Snaps, recipe page 179)

1 cup plus 2 tablespoons all-purpose flour

2 teaspoons grated orange zest

½ cup shelled pistachios, toasted and finely ground

1 teaspoon ground cinnamon

½ teaspoon freshly ground white pepper

½ cup unsalted butter

¼ cup sugar

1 egg white

4 ounces bittersweet chocolate, coarsely chopped

Do Ahead { The uncoated cookies can be frozen, tightly wrapped, for up to 1 month. The chocolate-coated cookies can be made up to 2 days ahead, stored in a single layer in an airtight container, and refrigerated.

Toss together the flour, orange zest, nuts, and spices. Set aside. With an electric mixer fitted with the paddle attachment, beat the butter until light, about 5 minutes. With the mixer running, add the sugar and beat well; add the egg white and beat until the mixture is light and fluffy, another 2 to 3 minutes. Add the flour mixture, one third at a time, until a smooth dough is formed, about 3 minutes. Put half of the dough on a piece of parchment paper; cover with another piece of parchment paper. With a rolling pin, roll out the dough ⅛ inch thick. Repeat with the other half of the dough. Refrigerate until firm, about 1 hour.

Preheat an oven to 325°. Transfer the dough from the refrigerator to a work surface; remove the top sheet of parchment paper. With cookie cutters, cut the dough into 2-inch rounds or into desired shapes. Remove the cut shapes from the parchment and put on an ungreased cookie sheet. Bake until lightly golden, 12 to 14 minutes. Remove from the oven and cool completely.

Melt the chocolate in a microwave or in the top of a double boiler over hot water. Dip the top of each cookie into the melted chocolate and place, chocolate side up, on a piece of waxed paper. Allow the chocolate to harden, about ½ hour.

Use unsalted butter unless otherwise specified for baking, as you don't want to add too much salt. Salted butter sometimes has a higher water content than unsalted butter, which can make a difference in the quality of the final product.

Caramel~Coated Yam Flan

Roxsand Scocos

Serves 8 to 10

The caramel adds a lovely texture and flavor to the flan, but the flan is also delicious on its own. The vanilla bean adds a subtle flavor, but in a pinch 1 teaspoon of pure vanilla extract will do.

Caramel

2 cups granulated sugar

2 cups water

Flan

4 cups heavy cream

1 vanilla bean

2 cinnamon sticks

1 pound yams, baked, peeled, and puréed

¾ cup granulated sugar

¾ cup firmly packed brown sugar

1 tablespoon ground cinnamon

1½ teaspoons ground allspice

1½ teaspoons ground cloves

6 eggs

6 egg yolks

2 tablespoons dark rum

2 tablespoons Kahlua

Do Ahead { The caramel and the flan can be made a day ahead, covered, and refrigerated.

For the caramel: Combine the sugar and 1¼ cups water in a heavy saucepan. Cook over medium heat without stirring until the sugar is melted. Increase the heat to medium-high and cook until the mixture is dark amber, swirling the pan occasionally. Pour about 1 cup of the caramel into an 11 x 7-inch baking dish and swirl around so the caramel completely covers the bottom and sides, adding more caramel if necessary. Set the caramel-lined pan aside to cool. Add ¾ cup water to the remaining caramel in the saucepan. Bring to a boil over medium-high heat and cook until the caramel dissolves and the mixture is smooth. Refrigerate or set aside at room temperature.

For the flan: Place the cream in a medium saucepan. With a sharp knife, slice the vanilla bean in half lengthwise, scrape the soft interior into the cream, then add the split bean and the cinnamon sticks. Place the pan over medium heat and bring just to a boil; remove the pan from the heat and allow the cream to steep for an hour. Let cool, then strain the cream mixture into a large bowl.

Preheat an oven to 325°. Place the caramel-lined baking dish on a baking sheet with 2-inch sides or in a pan roomy enough to hold the baking dish and water for a water bath (bain marie).

Add the remaining flan ingredients to the cream mixture and whisk until smooth. Strain the mixture into the prepared baking dish. Pour water into the baking sheet or pan so it comes halfway up the sides of the flan; bake until the center is firm but still jiggles a little, about 1 hour and 15 minutes. Remove from the oven and allow to cool in the water bath. Once cool, cover with plastic wrap and chill completely.

To serve, reheat the caramel sauce over medium heat. Place generous spoonsful of chilled flan into individual serving bowls and drizzle with the hot caramel. Serve immediately.

The deeper the color, the more flavorful the caramel. But always keep in mind that the mixture continues to caramelize even after it's removed from the heat.

Apple Wrap
Vincent Guerithault

Before he moved to Arizona, this French chef would never think of using tortillas in such an elegant way. But Vincent quickly discovered their versatility. This delicious apple dessert will remind you of crêpes, but they taste like the Southwest.

2 Granny Smith apples, peeled, cored, and thinly sliced
2 tablespoons granulated sugar
2 teaspoons ground cinnamon
4 flour tortillas, 8 inches in diameter
3 tablespoons confectioners' sugar
2 tablespoons unsalted butter
Whipped cream, crème fraîche, or ice cream, for accompaniment

In a bowl, gently toss together the apple slices, sugar, and cinnamon; allow to sit for 1 hour.

Preheat an oven to 375°.

Lay the tortillas out on a work surface; lightly sprinkle both sides with 2 tablespoons of the confectioners' sugar. Divide the apple mixture evenly among the tortillas, placing the filling down the center of each. Roll up the tortillas around the filling and place, seam side down, on a baking sheet. Bake until the tortillas start to brown, about 15 minutes. Remove from the oven and sprinkle with the remaining tablespoon of confectioners' sugar. Serve immediately with whipped cream, crème fraîche, or ice cream.

Chilied Fruit

Serves 8 to 10

A light, simple fruit dessert like this one is a delightful way to end a heavy meal. The chiltepín adds an unexpected bite when combined with the sugar and vinegar. Native Americans used this wild chile for cooking and as an aid in childbirth: They crushed the chile under the nose of a woman in labor to make her sneeze and push the baby out.

⅓ cup raspberry vinegar
¼ cup sugar
1 chiltepín
2 cups cubed cantaloupe
2 cups cubed honeydew
2 cups sliced fresh strawberries

Do Ahead { The longer the mixture sits, the hotter it gets, so this dessert should probably be made no more than 4 hours ahead.

Combine the vinegar and sugar in a small saucepan; stir over medium heat until the sugar is dissolved. Crush the chile into the mixture and let cool.

Gently toss the fruit together in a large glass bowl. Pour the vinegar mixture over the fruit and chill until ready to serve.

Texas Pecan Pie

Robert Del Grande

Pecans are abundant in the Southwest, particularly in Texas, which produces them by the bushel. Houston's Robert Del Grande created this delectable pie to show off the Lone Star State's favorite nut.

Dough

1¾ cups all-purpose flour
10 tablespoons chilled unsalted
  butter, cut into ½-inch pieces
¼ teaspoon salt
2 tablespoons ice water

Custard Filling

1 egg yolk
3 whole eggs
¾ cup firmly packed dark brown
  sugar
3 tablespoons butter, melted
1 cup light corn syrup
¼ teaspoon salt
1 tablespoon Grand Marnier

1½ cups pecan pieces

Do Ahead { The dough can be prepared up to 3 days ahead and refrigerated.

For the dough: Sift the flour into a bowl. Using a pastry cutter, 2 forks, or your fingertips, cut the butter into the flour until the mixture resembles coarse meal. Add the salt. Add the ice water and toss gently with a fork until a dough forms. If the dough is dry, add more ice water, 1 tablespoon at a time, until the dough comes together. Press the dough into a disc, wrap in plastic wrap, and chill thoroughly for at least 2 hours or up to 3 days in the refrigerator.

Remove the dough from the refrigerator. Dust a work surface with flour. Working quickly with a rolling pin, roll out the dough into a circle 15 inches in diameter. Line an 11-inch tart pan with a removable bottom with the dough, pressing the dough evenly into the pan and trimming the edges. Return the lined tart pan to the refrigerator and chill for at least 2 hours or overnight.

For the custard filling: In a medium bowl, whisk together the egg yolk, eggs, and dark brown sugar. Add the melted butter, corn syrup, salt, and Grand Marnier. Whisk until smooth.

Assembly: Preheat an oven to 325°. Sprinkle the pecan pieces over the bottom of the chilled tart shell. Pour the custard over the top of the pecans. Bake until the filling has set, 35 to 45 minutes. Let cool completely and serve.

Peach and Cherry Crumble

Serves 6 to 8

Peaches are grown throughout the Southwest and even have historic and symbolic significance to the Navajo nation. Their crops, including their prized peach orchards in Canyon de Chelly, were destroyed by Kit Carson's men in 1864. The orchards were replanted and once again flourish. Make this dessert when the fruit is at its peak of flavor. If cherries are not in season, substitute blueberries, blackberries, or raspberries.

Fruit Filling

1½ pounds peaches, pitted and
   cut into ½-inch-thick wedges
   (about 4 cups)
½ pound cherries, pitted and
   halved (about 1¼ cups)
1½ tablespoons freshly
   squeezed lemon juice
1 teaspoon grated lemon zest
½ cup granulated sugar

Topping

½ cup whole-wheat flour
¼ cup firmly packed light brown
   sugar
½ cup rolled oats
¼ teaspoon salt
1 teaspoon ground cinnamon
½ teaspoon freshly grated
   nutmeg
6 tablespoons unsalted butter,
   cut into bits, chilled

Ice cream, for accompaniment

For the fruit filling: In a large bowl, toss the peaches and cherries with the lemon juice, lemon zest, and granulated sugar until the mixture is well combined. Allow to sit for at least 30 minutes.

For the topping: In a small bowl, stir together the flour, brown sugar, rolled oats, salt, cinnamon, and nutmeg. Add the butter; cut into the dry mixture with a fork.

Assembly and baking: Preheat an oven to 375°. Butter an 8 x 8-inch square baking dish.

With a slotted spoon, remove the fruit from any liquid that's accumulated and spread it over the bottom of the prepared baking dish. Sprinkle the dry topping mixture evenly over the fruit; bake in the middle of the oven for 30 minutes. Increase heat to 400° and bake 5 minutes more. Remove from the oven.

Let the crumble cool for 45 to 60 minutes before serving. Serve with ice cream.

Goat Cheese Pound Cake with Blackberry Crisp

Robert Del Grande

From the dessert menu at Cafe Annie comes a new take on the homey fruit crumble. It's a perfect balance of flavors and textures. The pound cake isn't overly sweet, and leftovers make out-of-this-world breakfast toast.

Pound Cake

1 cup sugar

1 cup unsalted butter, cut into small pieces

4 ounces mild goat cheese (about ½ cup)

1 tablespoon pure vanilla extract

6 eggs, separated

1½ cups all-purpose flour

1 teaspoon baking powder

1 teaspoon salt

Crisp Topping

1 cup flour

¾ cup firmly packed light brown sugar

½ teaspoon salt

½ teaspoon ground cinnamon

½ cup cold unsalted butter, cut into small pieces

4 cups fresh blackberries

2 tablespoons all-purpose flour

2 tablespoons granulated sugar

6 tablespoons heavy cream

For the pound cake: Preheat an oven to 300°. Butter a 9 x 5-inch loaf pan (6-cup capacity).

In a large bowl, beat the sugar and butter on low speed with an electric mixer fitted with the paddle attachment until the butter is light and creamy, 10 to 15 minutes. Add the goat cheese and vanilla and mix well to incorporate, about 1 minute more. With the mixer running, add egg yolks, one at a time, until fluffy and fully incorporated, about 5 minutes. In a separate bowl, stir together the flour, baking powder, and salt. Slowly add the flour mixture to the butter-egg mixture and mix just until combined. Do not overmix.

With a balloon whisk, whip the whites until they hold soft peaks. Fold one-third of the whites into the cake batter to lighten it. Then fold in the remaining egg whites. Pour the batter into the prepared pan and bake until a toothpick inserted into the center comes out clean, about 1 hour. Remove from the oven and cool.

For the crisp topping: In a bowl, stir together the flour, brown sugar, salt, and cinnamon; mix well. Add the pieces of butter and, with your fingers, a pastry blender, or an electric mixer, mix until the ingredients form a moist, coarse dough. Reserve.

Assembly and baking: Cut 5 or 6 slices (each ½ inch thick) from the cooled pound cake. Lightly toast the slices in a toaster or a preheated broiler. Break the toasted slices into quarters and arrange them in a tight single layer in the bottom of an 11 x 7-inch glass baking dish. (There's enough pound cake to make two desserts; use the extra for another dessert or freeze for up to 1 month.)

Preheat an oven to 350°.

In a bowl, combine the blackberries, flour, and granulated sugar; toss lightly. Carefully distribute the berry mixture evenly over the toasted pound cake. Sprinkle any flour-sugar mixture left in the bowl over the berries. In a fine stream, drizzle the cream over the berries. Crumble the crisp topping over the blackberries. Bake until the topping is crisp, 45 to 50 minutes. Let cool for 15 minutes. Serve warm.

Arizona Princess Cake

Donna Nordin

Serves 12

In honor of her adopted state, Arizona, Donna created this rich, dense confection with such good regional tastes as pecans and tequila. Donna was a chocolate expert before moving to the Southwest, and traveled and did demonstrations for the Ghirardelli company of San Francisco.

Cake

½ cup minced dried apples
(about 1½ ounces)
⅓ cup tequila
8 ounces bittersweet chocolate,
chopped
½ cup unsalted butter
3 eggs, separated
⅔ cup sugar
¼ cup all-purpose flour
⅔ cup toasted pecans, finely
chopped

Glaze

8 ounces bittersweet chocolate,
chopped
½ cup unsalted butter
1 tablespoon light corn syrup

Decoration

½ cup chopped toasted pecans
12 pecan halves

Do Ahead { The cake can be prepared 4 days ahead. Refrigerate and bring to room temperature before glazing. The glazed cake can be prepared 1 day ahead; refrigerate and let stand at room temperature for 3 hours before serving.

For the cake: Combine the apples and tequila in a small bowl; let stand 30 minutes.

Preheat an oven to 375°. Butter an 8-inch round cake pan; line the bottom with parchment paper. Dust the pan sides lightly with flour; tap out excess.

In a microwave or in a double boiler, melt the chocolate and butter; stir until smooth.

In a large bowl with an electric mixer, beat the egg yolks with ⅓ cup of the sugar at high speed until pale yellow and a ribbon forms when beaters are lifted, about 5 minutes. Mix in the chocolate mixture and flour, then the pecans. Add the apples and any unabsorbed tequila.

Using clean, dry beaters, beat the egg whites until soft peaks form. Gradually add the remaining ⅓ cup sugar and beat until stiff and shiny. Fold one-third of the whites into the chocolate mixture to lighten, then fold in the remaining whites.

Pour the batter into the prepared pan and bake until the cake pulls away from the sides of the pan and a tester inserted 2 inches from the center of the cake comes out clean, about 40 minutes. Let cake cool in the pan (it will sink as it cools). Press down gently on the edges of the cake to even.

For the glaze: Melt the chocolate and butter with the corn syrup in a microwave or in a double boiler, stirring frequently until smooth. Let cool until thick enough to spread, about 10 minutes.

Invert the cooled cake onto an 8-inch cardboard round. Peel the parchment paper off the bottom of the cake and set the cake on a rack over a baking sheet. Spread a very thin coat of glaze over the top and sides of the cake. Refrigerate the cake for 10 minutes.

Rewarm the remaining glaze until just pourable. Strain the glaze over the cake, spreading quickly with a spatula. Let stand until the glaze is almost set. Press the chopped nuts onto the sides of the cake; arrange the pecan halves around the top edge. Transfer to a platter. Serve at room temperature.

Chapter

8

Sauces, Salsas, and Relishes

Across New Mexico in the late fall, ripe scarlet chiles hang in decorative garlands—*ristras*—at every front door. In the heat of the autumn sun—nature's drying oven—the chiles shrivel, their color deepens, their flavor intensifies. No longer fresh and subject to spoiling, the chiles take on new purpose as a long-lasting pantry spice.

To generations of resourceful cooks faced with the slim pickings of winter, these brilliant strings were more than a harvest symbol. They gave taste appeal to the simple fare of a barren season. As such, they've also proved a life-sustaining food. Storing a foot of ristra per family member to make it through the cold months is an old rule of thumb.

Dried chiles are indispensable to the Southwest's ubiquitous red sauce, that classic companion to its most famous traditional dishes from enchiladas to huevos rancheros to tacos. In the hands of modern

Southwestern chefs like Mary Sue Milliken and Susan Feniger, this staple seasoning finds a new showcase in such intriguing creations as Chipotle-Corn Relish (see page 210), Vegetarian Red Bean Chili (see page 76), and Ancho-Glazed Chicken (see page 94).

You can buy dried chiles now right off the supermarket shelf, from the fruity, sweet mahogany ancho to the raisinlike pasilla to the earthy, brick red New Mexico. They're so crucial to Southwestern cuisine that when they change their form from fresh to dried, sometimes their name changes, too: The ancho is a dried poblano chile, while the chipotle began as a jalapeño. Shop for them a few times and you'll catch on.

Dried chiles, like dried mushrooms, are a different ingredient altogether than their fresh form, more complex, and for their size, much more potent. Each has a unique personality that with some experimenting you'll get to know. Then the fun begins as you orchestrate their different flavors to give old recipe standbys new personality.

This chapter includes a traditional red sauce that gets its fire from ten whole dried New Mexico chiles. Dried chiles appear in many of the other foundation sauces and salsas as well. If you've never cooked with dried chiles, you couldn't find a better launching pad for your exploration of the Southwest's most famous spice than the examples that follow. If you're an experienced chilehead, jump right in and join the party.

Mango~Chipotle Barbecue Sauce

Lenard Rubin

Makes 4 cups

This delicious, complex sauce is brushed on Lenard's Barbecued Beef Short Ribs (see page 84) during the last hour of cooking to create some of the best barbecue you'll ever eat. It would work equally well for chicken or pork.

1 mango, peeled, pitted, and
 cut into cubes
2 tablespoons water
1 tablespoon plus ¼ cup
 freshly squeezed lemon juice
1¾ cups tomato ketchup
1¾ cups honey
1 tablespoon curry powder
1 tablespoon chile powder
3 tablespoons chopped onion
2 tablespoons chopped garlic
1 tablespoon freshly ground
 black pepper
1 teaspoon cayenne pepper
3 tablespoons soy sauce
¼ cup Worcestershire sauce
1 teaspoon Tabasco sauce
2 tablespoons adobo sauce
 from canned chipotle chiles
1 jalapeño chile, seeded and
 chopped
½ cup chopped cilantro

Do Ahead { The sauce keeps, tightly covered, in the refrigerator for up to 1 week.

Place the mango, water, and 1 tablespoon lemon juice in a blender and purée. Scrape into a saucepan and add the remaining ingredients. Bring the mixture to a boil over medium-high heat; reduce the heat and simmer for 20 minutes. Transfer the mixture back into the blender and purée until smooth. Pour back into the saucepan and bring to a boil over medium heat; simmer for another 20 minutes. Remove from the heat and cool.

Chipotle Sauce

Mary Sue Milliken and
Susan Feniger

Makes 3 cups

This wonderfully earthy, slightly smoky red chile sauce will give a whole new dimension to any recipe that calls for one, from enchiladas to tacos to huevos rancheros to a hearty stew. The sauce adds real flavor to Mary Sue and Susan's Smoky Fideo Soup (page 64) and to Seafood Stew (see page 69).

¾ ounce dried chipotle chiles
(about 6 to 8) or ¼ cup
canned chipotle chiles,
stemmed

5 ripe plum tomatoes, cored

7 cloves garlic

4 cups water

1 tablespoon salt

½ teaspoon freshly ground black
pepper

Do Ahead { Chipotle sauce can be stored, covered, in the refrigerator up to 5 days, or frozen.

Combine all of the ingredients in a saucepan and bring to a boil over high heat. Reduce to a simmer and cook, uncovered, until the liquid is reduced by one-third and the skins fall off the tomatoes, about 20 minutes. Set aside to cool.

Pour the mixture into a blender or food processor fitted with the metal blade. Purée until smooth. Strain into a clean bowl and refrigerate. Serve chilled.

Green Chile and Tomatillo Sauce

Makes 2 cups

This spicy, tangy sauce is delicious over grilled chicken or fish, mixed with vegetables in tamales, or spooned on scrambled eggs to give the morning meal a wake-up call. When you're bored with red sauce, try this on huevos rancheros.

4 tomatillos, husked, washed, and diced

1½ cups chicken stock

1 tablespoon vegetable oil

1 clove garlic, chopped

½ cup chopped green onions, white and light green parts, about 1 bunch

½ cup long green chiles, roasted, peeled, seeded, and diced

¼ cup chopped cilantro

1 tablespoon freshly squeezed lime juice

1 teaspoon ground cumin

Salt and freshly ground black pepper to taste

Do Ahead { The sauce can be refrigerated, covered, up to 3 days. Reheat before serving.

In a saucepan over medium heat, bring the tomatillos and chicken stock to a boil. Reduce the heat and simmer until the liquid is reduced to ¾ cup, about 15 minutes.

In a small skillet, heat the vegetable oil. Sauté the garlic and onions over medium heat until soft, 5 to 10 minutes.

In a blender, combine the tomatillo-stock mixture, sautéed garlic and onions, green chiles, cilantro, lime juice, and cumin. Purée and add salt and pepper to taste. Serve immediately.

Stockpile chiles in season in the freezer so you can make this versatile sauce at any time of year. Roast the fresh chiles first, then clean them or not (in fact, they peel even easier after freezing) before you freeze them in airtight plastic bags.

Red Bell Pepper Ketchup

Robert McGrath

Makes about 1½ cups

There's ketchup from the squeeze bottle, and then there's Robert's delectable spread, an entirely different food altogether. You can make it in minutes to slather as usual on hamburgers, French fries, and meat loaf (they've never tasted better). But it's also special enough to season more upscale foods. Robert stirs it into the sauce for his Sugar- and Chile-Cured Duck Breasts (see page 99).

2 teaspoons olive oil
1 tablespoon finely chopped
   onion
2 tablespoons malt vinegar
2 tablespoons water
1 tablespoon molasses
4 red bell peppers, roasted,
   peeled, seeded, and puréed
   (about 1 cup)
2 teaspoons brown sugar
½ teaspoon salt
¼ teaspoon cayenne pepper

Do Ahead { The ketchup can be made up to 1 week ahead of time, covered, and refrigerated.

In a heavy skillet, heat the olive oil over medium heat until hot. Add the onion and sauté until softened, about 3 minutes. Add the vinegar, water, and molasses and simmer for 2 to 3 minutes. Add the roasted pepper purée, brown sugar, salt, and cayenne pepper. Cook until the sugar is dissolved and all the ingredients are well blended, about 3 minutes. Adjust seasonings to taste.

Red Sauce

One of the foundation sauces for Mexican and Southwest cuisine, red sauce is excellent for enchiladas, huevos rancheros, tamales, and meats. A few tablespoons stirred into soups, stews, or beans, adds extra zip. Dried red New Mexico chiles are also commonly used as crushed flakes and chile powders.

10 whole dried New Mexico chiles, stemmed and seeded
1 tablespoon olive oil
1 cup finely chopped onion
2 cloves garlic, finely chopped
2 cups chicken stock
2 tablespoons vegetable oil or lard
Salt to taste

Do Ahead { The sauce can be made up to 3 days ahead of time, covered, and refrigerated or frozen.

Preheat a heavy skillet over medium heat. Open the chiles and toast them, in batches if necessary, in the dry skillet for 3 to 4 minutes, being careful not to let them burn. In the meantime, fill a pot just large enough to hold the chiles with water. Bring the water a boil and remove the pot from the heat. Add the toasted chiles to the hot water and, using a weight such as the lid to the pot, keep them submerged until they are soft, about 20 or 30 minutes. Drain the chiles.

Heat the olive oil in a medium skillet over low heat. Add the onion and sauté until browned.

Place the drained chiles, sautéed onion, garlic, and 1 cup chicken stock into a blender or food processor. Purée until smooth.

Heat the vegetable oil in a heavy skillet over medium heat. Strain the chile mixture into the hot oil and cook, stirring, for about 5 minutes. Add more chicken stock until the sauce is the desired consistency. Add salt to taste. Keep refrigerated until ready to use.

To prepare dried chiles for toasting: Cut off the stem with a sharp knife, then slit the chile down one side. Open it up and shake out the seeds. It doesn't matter if all the seeds aren't removed at this stage; they will be strained off later on.

Salsa Fresca

Janos Wilder

The success of this uncooked salsa depends on good ingredients. Use the best ripe red tomatoes you can find. Janos uses 25 different types of tomatoes in the summer at his restaurant—a far cry from the early days when it first opened and he couldn't get any good tomatoes at all. To ensure a steady supply, Janos hired gardeners before any other restaurant staff!

As the final touch to his Blue Corn–Crusted Cabrilla (see page 112), Janos tops it with this version of a classic fresh salsa. It's also scrumptious on quesadillas, nachos, tacos, or plain tortilla chips. (Pictured page 201)

4 ripe tomatoes, seeded and
   diced
½ cup diced red onion
½ cup finely chopped green
   onion
1 long green chile, roasted,
   peeled, seeded, and finely
   chopped
½ cup chopped cilantro
1 tablespoon finely chopped
   garlic
1 tablespoon balsamic vinegar
1 tablespoon red wine vinegar
1 tablespoon olive oil
Salt and freshly ground black
   pepper to taste

Do Ahead { This salsa can be made up to 8 hours ahead and refrigerated.

In a large bowl, combine all the ingredients. Serve at room temperature, or refrigerate and serve chilled.

198 Savor the Southwest

Three~Tomato Pico

Stephan Pyles

Makes about 3 cups

This new twist on a traditional salsa incorporates nontraditional yellow tomatoes and tangy green tomatillos. Medium-hot serrano chiles are used here, but you can crank up or lower the heat by varying their amount. But, says chef Stephan Pyles: "If it's too hot, you've done something wrong. Chiles should be used to season, not to blow your palate away."

Stephan spoons this relish on his Goat Cheese and Crab Rellenos (see page 108), but he also suggests it as a garnish for any grilled fish, meat, or poultry, with eggs, or with chips. (Pictured page 201)

2 ripe tomatoes, outer flesh only, cut into ¼-inch dice

2 yellow tomatoes, outer flesh only, cut into ¼-inch dice

2 tomatillos, husked, washed, and cut into ¼-inch dice

1 tablespoon chopped cilantro

1 clove garlic, finely chopped

½ cup finely chopped onion

1 tablespoon freshly squeezed lime juice

2 small serrano chiles, stemmed, seeded, and finely chopped

Salt to taste

Do Ahead { This salsa can be made up to 4 hours ahead.

In a nonreactive bowl, combine all the ingredients. Let stand at least 30 minutes before serving so the flavors can blend. Serve at room temperature, or refrigerate and serve chilled.

Tomatillo Salsa

Janos Wilder

Makes 2 cups

Lemony tomatillos are also known as Mexican green tomatoes, but while they're in the same nightshade family, they're not tomatoes at all. They have a papery husk around light green skin and flesh, and they should be firm to the touch (they don't soften when ripe). More often they're cooked in a sauce, but here they're used raw to give some acidity to this fresh salsa.

Janos tops his Lobster and Corn Enchiladas (see page 106) with this tangy salsa, which cuts through some of the richness of the dish. (Pictured right, with Salsa Fresca, recipe page 198, and Three-Tomato Pico, recipe page 199)

12 tomatillos, husked, washed, and coarsely chopped

1 cup coarsely chopped yellow onion

1 serrano chile, stemmed and seeded

1 tablespoon chopped garlic

1 cup finely chopped green onions, white and light green parts

½ cup chopped cilantro

1 teaspoon olive oil

Salt and freshly ground black pepper to taste

Do Ahead { The tomatillos, yellow onion, chile, and garlic can be puréed together a day ahead of time, but add the green onions, cilantro, and olive oil just before serving.

Place the tomatillos, onion, chile, and garlic in the bowl of a food processor; pulse until coarsely puréed. Scrape the mixture into a nonreactive bowl and fold in the green onions, cilantro, and oil. Add salt and pepper to taste and refrigerate until ready to serve.

Dried Cherry Salsa

Makes about 1½ cups

The dried cherries are the only "import" in this otherwise all-Southwestern salsa. The other main ingredients are grown in the region. The cherries give the salsa a slightly chewy texture and another layer of fruit. Serve this colorful, toothsome relish with any pork dish for a winning combination.

¼ cup freshly squeezed orange
   juice
¼ cup sugar
½ cup coarsely chopped dried
   cherries
¼ cup coarsely chopped toasted
   pecans
1 red bell pepper, roasted,
   peeled, seeded, and diced
1 Anaheim chile, roasted, peeled,
   seeded, and diced
1 tablespoon grated orange zest
¼ cup chopped cilantro
Salt and freshly ground black
   pepper to taste

Do Ahead { The salsa can be made a day ahead of time without the cilantro; add the cilantro just before serving.

In a small heavy pan over medium heat, bring the orange juice and sugar to a boil, stirring occasionally. Lower the heat and simmer until the sugar is dissolved. Remove from the heat and add the dried cherries. Allow to steep for 1 hour.

In a nonreactive bowl, stir together the remaining ingredients; add the cherry mixture and salt and pepper.

Papaya Salsa

Makes about 2 cups

Fruit is a delicious foil to the punch of a chile, which is why so many cuisines—the Southwest included—pair sweet with a little heat. This textbook salsa rates an A for its mix of colors, textures, and tastes. It's especially good with grilled chicken or a fresh-caught trout.

1 papaya, peeled, seeded, and diced
1 red bell pepper, cored, seeded, and diced
1 serrano chile, stemmed, seeded, and diced
¼ cup finely chopped red onion
1 tablespoon finely chopped cilantro
1 tablespoon freshly squeezed lime juice
1 teaspoon grated lime zest
Salt and freshly ground black pepper to taste

Do Ahead { The salsa can be made without the cilantro up to 4 hours ahead of time, covered, and refrigerated. Add the cilantro just before serving.

Combine all the ingredients in a nonreactive bowl. Allow to stand for 1 hour before serving to allow the flavors to mellow. Serve on grilled fish, poultry, or meats, with cheese quesadillas, or with chips.

Don't skimp on the salt in this recipe, even if it sounds odd to include it. It brings up all the flavors.

Mexican Cream

Makes 1 cup

This tangy Mexican sauce, which has a refreshing hint of lime, is used like crème fraîche or sour cream. You can find it in Latino markets and many supermarkets throughout the Southwest, but it's easier and cheaper to make your own. For more punch as a sauce or to drizzle on soups, swirl in a puréed chipotle chile.

½ cup heavy cream
½ cup sour cream
1 teaspoon freshly squeezed lime juice

Do Ahead { The cream keeps in the refrigerator, tightly covered, for up to 1 week.

In a nonreactive bowl, whisk together the cream, sour cream, and lime juice. Cover with plastic wrap and refrigerate for at least 2 hours.

Chipotle Mayonnaise

Makes 1 cup

Substitute this spread for your usual mayonnaise and your sandwiches will really sing. It boosts Grilled Potato Salad (see page 48) from tasty to totally irresistible. Store any leftover chipotle chiles in a glass jar in the refrigerator up to 1 month, or freeze them.

1 cup mayonnaise
1 tablespoon freshly squeezed
   lime juice
2 chipotle chiles in adobo sauce,
   puréed and strained
1 teaspoon ground cumin
Salt and freshly ground black
   pepper to taste

Do Ahead { The mayonnaise keeps for up to 1 week, covered, in the refrigerator.

Combine all ingredients in a nonreactive bowl. Cover and refrigerate.

Tomato Preserves

Loretta Barrett Oden   ### Makes about 2 cups

Tomatoes are one of the indigenous foods of the Americas, a specialty of Loretta's Corn Dance Cafe in Santa Fe, New Mexico. Contrary to conventional wisdom, canned tomatoes have their place in cooking, and these tasty, no-work preserves are one of them. Not all canned products are equally good, though, so sample a number of them until you find one that you like.

Loretta spoons this thick, chunky mixture on Skillet Corn Cake (see page 126), but it would also be great on grilled corn bread or tortillas.

1 (16-ounce) can diced tomatoes
1 cup sugar
1 teaspoon ground cloves

Do Ahead { The preserves can be made up to 1 week ahead, covered, and refrigerated.

Place all the ingredients in a heavy saucepan. Place over low heat, bring to a simmer, and cook, stirring frequently, until cooked down and thickened, about 1 hour. Remove from the heat and cool. Place in jars and keep refrigerated.

Achiote Paste

Chuck Wiley

Makes about 1 cup

Use this variation of a traditional Yucatán spice paste on grilled meats or stir it into a stew as a delicious seasoning. Amber achiote (or annatto) seeds are a key ingredient for the golden hue they impart and their subtle flavor. Roasted ancho chiles add an intriguing chocolate-apricot scent as well as some heat. Commercial achiote paste is sold in Latino markets, but it is powdery and needs a liquid or fat added to it to release its earthy, slightly spicy taste. Achiote seeds are available in Latino or specialty markets or by mail order (see Mail-Order Sources, page 217).

3 ancho chiles
1 clove garlic
¼ teaspoon ground allspice
½ teaspoon cumin seeds, toasted and crushed
1 teaspoon achiote (annatto) seeds
1 teaspoon olive oil
2 tablespoons white wine vinegar
¼ cup freshly squeezed orange juice
½ teaspoon salt

Do Ahead { The paste keeps up to 1 week in the refrigerator.

Toast the ancho chiles in a heavy skillet over medium-high heat until oil is released and they smell toasted, 2 to 3 minutes. Cool slightly, stem, seed, and tear into strips. Place the strips in a blender with the remaining ingredients; purée until smooth. Cover and refrigerate for at least 24 hours, allowing the flavors to blend.

Pickled Chipotles

Mary Sue Milliken and Susan Feniger

Makes 2 cups

Whether chopped up in salsas or soups or downed whole, these eye-popping marinated chiles will make even hard-core chileheads sit up and take notice. Mary Sue and Susan use dried chipotle chiles, less common than canned chipotles in adobo sauce, but available from catalogs (see Mail-Order Sources, page 217) and some Latino markets.

The chefs incorporate both the pickled chipotles and the chile-infused red wine vinegar produced when you make them in their Chipotle-Corn Relish (see page 210). (Pictured right, with Southwest Spice Rub, recipe page 208)

6 dried chipotle or morita chiles, stemmed and seeded
2 cups red wine vinegar

Do Ahead { The pickled chiles will keep, in a tightly covered jar, in the refrigerator for up to 3 months.

Combine the chiles and vinegar in a small saucepan and bring to a boil over high heat. Reduce to a simmer and cook, covered, for 5 minutes. Set aside to cool.

Southwest Spice Rub

Makes about ⅓ cup

Rub this lively mixture on pork or beef before grilling, toss a little in a salad for extra flavor, or add to a soup that needs some kick. With its peppery jolt and brick red hue, it's the Southwest in a jar and makes a great gift for a chile-loving host. (Pictured page 207)

2 teaspoons cumin seed
2 teaspoons whole coriander
  seed
2 tablespoons chile powder
2 teaspoons sugar
1 teaspoon salt
1 teaspoon black peppercorns
½ teaspoon cayenne pepper

Do Ahead { The spice rub will keep in a glass jar in a cool, dry place for up to 1 month.

Place the cumin seed in a small dry skillet over medium-high heat and toast until lightly browned and aromatic. Transfer to a mini food processor, coffee grinder, or spice grinder and purée. Toast the coriander in the same skillet and add to the cumin in the grinder. Purée again. Add the remaining ingredients and purée until well blended.

For a healthier version of tortilla chips, bake them—don't fry them—and sprinkle them with Southwest spice rub. Cut tortillas in strips, lightly coat them with nonstick cooking spray, and sprinkle with rub. Bake the chips at 350° until crisp, about 10 minutes.

Ancho Chile Relish

Mary Sue Milliken and Susan Feniger

Makes about 1 cup

Spoon this relish over a big bowl of beans or chili. Its fresh, crunchy flavor makes a pleasing contrast to the rich beans. Select anchos that are pliable, not old and brittle, and store unused chiles in the freezer in an airtight bag.

6 ancho chiles, wiped clean, stemmed, and seeded

1 cup freshly squeezed orange juice

⅓ cup freshly squeezed grapefruit juice

3 tablespoons freshly squeezed lime juice

1½ teaspoons salt

½ teaspoon freshly ground black pepper

4 tablespoons extra virgin olive oil

3 green onions, white and light green parts, thinly sliced on the diagonal

Do Ahead { Ancho chile relish can be made a few days ahead, then stored covered, in the refrigerator, without the green onions. Add the green onions just before serving.

Toast the chiles directly over a medium gas flame or in a cast-iron skillet until soft and brown, turning frequently to avoid scorching. Slice the chiles into 1-inch strips, then into very fine julienne. Combine the chiles, juices, salt, pepper, and olive oil in a nonreactive bowl; mix well and let sit at least 30 minutes or as long as 2 hours before serving. Stir in the green onions just before serving.

Juice an orange, lemon, or lime with just a fork: Halve the fruit and dig a fork into the center of the flesh of one of the halves. Hold the fork steady in one hand, and with your other hand, twist the fruit to release the juice. Easy and no equipment to clean.

Chipotle~Corn Relish

Mary Sue Milliken and Susan Feniger

Makes about 4 cups

Newly minted vegetarians who still have a yen for bacon will especially love this fresh relish because the chipotle chiles have a similar smoky taste. It's a great match with tortilla chips, grilled chicken, or pork. Chipotle vinegar is a tasty by-product of pickling your own chipotles (see page 206). Mary Sue and Susan pair their crunchy condiment with Ancho-Glazed Chicken (see page 94).

¼ cup olive oil
2 cups corn kernels (3 or 4 ears)
1 teaspoon salt
¾ teaspoon freshly ground black
    pepper
1 avocado, peeled and seeded
1 large red bell pepper, cored,
    seeded, and cut into ¼-inch
    dice
3 green onions, white and light
    green parts, thinly sliced on
    the diagonal
1 to 2 pickled chipotle chiles,
    seeded and minced
¼ cup chipotle or red wine
    vinegar

Do Ahead

The relish can be stored, tightly covered, in the refrigerator up to 1 day. To make 2 to 3 days in advance, mix all the ingredients except for the avocado and store in the refrigerator. Add the avocado shortly before serving.

Heat 2 tablespoons of the olive oil in a large skillet over medium heat. Add the corn, salt, and pepper and sauté until tender, about 5 minutes. Transfer to a large mixing bowl and set aside to cool.

Cut the avocado into ½-inch dice; add to the bowl with the corn. Add the bell pepper, green onions, chipotles, vinegar, and the remaining 2 tablespoons olive oil. Mix well and let sit 20 to 30 minutes to blend the flavors. Serve at room temperature.

Guacamole

Makes about 1½ cups

Ripe, creamy avocado is the prime ingredient in this luscious mixture and the inspiration for its name, which derives in part from the Aztec word for the pear-shaped tropical fruit. Guacamole is a staple of the Mexican and Southwestern table, but today its popularity transcends any borders. Spoon it on tacos, fajitas, cheese crisps, on quesadillas, or scoop it up with tortilla chips.

2 large ripe avocados
1 tablespoon freshly squeezed
   lime juice
1 ripe tomato, seeded and diced
2 green onions, white and light
   green parts, finely chopped
1 jalapeño chile, stemmed,
   seeded, and finely chopped
¼ cup sour cream
Salt to taste

Do Ahead { The guacamole can be made up to 4 hours ahead of time if stored in the refrigerator with plastic wrap pressed directly on the surface of the guacamole (air is what turns it brown).

Peel the avocados and remove the pits. With the back of a fork, mash the avocados with lime juice in a bowl. Stir in the tomato, green onions, jalapeño, and sour cream. Add salt to taste.

To slice a jalapeño chile, stand it on its tip and hold by the stem. With a sharp knife, slice down top to bottom slightly away from the stem to cut off one segment. Rotate by the stem and repeat until just the core, stem, and seeds are left. Use the flesh and discard the rest.

Glossary

Achiote Also called annatto, the tiny seeds of the tropical annatto tree are brick red and taste slightly musky. They are a common coloring for cheese, margarine, and butter. Mexican cooks combine them with chiles and other spices for seasoning pastes. Look for achiote—whole, powder, or paste—in Latino and specialty markets. To make Achiote Paste: See page 205.

Anasazi Beans The ancient, canyon-dwelling Anasazi Indians are thought to have first cultivated these mottled red-and-white beans. They were almost nonexistent until recently revived by groups dedicated to preserving such heirlooms. They're sold at specialty produce stores and natural food stores and taste similar to pintos.

Avocado It's not guacamole without this favorite Mexican ingredient and garnish. Ripe Haas avocados have a black, pebbly skin, with a dense, buttery flesh preferred for guacamole over the more watery green-skinned Fuertes variety. To ripen if hard: Enclose for 24 hours in a brown paper bag with a ripe banana. When soft, refrigerate up to 1 week. To halve: Slice lengthwise and twist open. To pit: Halve the avocado, then whack the pit with a chef's knife; pull out knife and pit together. To slice: With a sharp knife, slice the flesh in the shell; scoop out slices with a spoon. To dice: Cut into cubes in the shell, then scoop out.

Bell Peppers In the same family as hot chiles, but sweet, crunchy, and green, red, yellow, orange, even purple. To core and seed: Slice off both ends. Lay the pepper on its side and slit one side, top to bottom. Set skin side down, then cut away membranes and seeds by sliding the knife along the length of the flesh. To julienne: Slice into thin matchsticks (see **Julienne**). To dice: Cut into strips, then cut the strips crosswise into small to large cubes. To roast: See **Chiles, Fresh**.

Burro/Burrito A large, filled flour tortilla. To assemble: Lay the filling, usually shredded meat, chicken, or beans with cheese, down the center of the tortilla. Fold up the top and bottom of the tortilla, then one side. Roll until the filling is completely enclosed.

Chayote Squash Also called vegetable pear because of its shape, green chayote is native to Central America. Enjoy its mild white flesh—something like a cucumber—raw or cooked, as you would any squash. To prepare: Peel with a paring knife or vegetable peeler, then rinse off any viscous film left on the flesh. Chayote are most plentiful in winter.

Cheeses, Mexican You can find authentic Mexican cheeses at Latino markets, usually under the Cacique label, or at specialty stores with a good cheese section.

Cotija This crumbly, hard white cheese has a tangy, aged flavor like Parmesan. Feta or Monterey jack are substitutes.

Queso Blanco A slightly aged, mild white cheese that melts, but is otherwise considered a type of queso fresco. Use provolone as a substitute.

Queso Fresco Mexico's most popular cheese is white, slightly tangy, and nonmelting. It is usually crumbly like feta—an acceptable substitute—but it can vary in consistency.

Chiles, Dried Packed with intense, complex flavor, dried red chiles are a signature Southwest ingredient. Buy flexible, not brittle, dried chiles with bright, uniform color. Freeze them airtight for up to 6 months. To toast: For a deeper flavor, toast dried chiles in a heavy skillet over medium-high heat, 30 to 60 seconds per side (just until aromatic and more flexible). To reconstitute: Submerge a dried chile in boiling water (off the heat). Soak until soft and pliable, 15 to 20 minutes. Drain, remove the stems and seeds, and use as needed. To make pure chile powder: Remove the stems and seeds and grind to a powder in a mini food processor, spice or coffee grinder, blender, or with a mortar and pestle. Store in a cool, dry, dark spot and use quickly as it loses potency and flavor with time.

Ancho A dried poblano chile that is brick red to deep burgundy, wrinkled, and about 5 inches long by 3 inches wide. Sweeter than other dried chiles, it is mildly fruity and earthy. Pasillas, which are long and skinny, are sometimes incorrectly identified as anchos.

Cayenne Hot, pungent, and smoky, the bright red, tapered cayenne is usually ground into a seasoning powder. It measures 3 inches long by ½ inch wide.

Chiltepín Also called tepín and chile tepín, this tiny but fiercely hot wild red chile is round and about ½ inch across. Pequín, the cultivated form, is easier to find.

Chipotle A dried, smoked jalapeño, chipotles are sold both dried and canned in adobo sauce. About 3 inches long, chipotles are dark brown, with a subtle, smoky heat.

Morita A diminutive mora chile, both a form of dried, smoked jalapeño, the morita measures about 1½ inches long and a little over ¼ inch across. It is orange-to-brownish red, with a delicate, fruity flavor.

New Mexico This tapered chile, about 6 inches long, is also called chile colorado when red. The very versatile scarlet chile adds its crisp heat to sauces and its beauty to the decorative garlands known as ristras. It is also sold as a pure seasoning powder and as crushed flakes.

Pasilla A dried chilaca chile also called chile negro, the 6-inch-long pasilla is as wrinkled as a raisin and the same dark brown. It tastes like berries and is often mislabeled as an ancho, but they look nothing alike.

Chiles, Fresh In the genus *Capsicum*, fresh chiles range in size from as small as a pea to as large as a zucchini, and in color from green to vibrant shades of red and yellow. Select chiles that are dry, feel firm, and have shiny, unblemished skin. Store them, wrapped in paper towels (not in a plastic bag), in the refrigerator for several weeks. To handle fresh chiles: All chiles have the fiery compound capsaicin in their ribs and seeds that can burn your face and eyes. Wear disposable gloves, especially with the fiercest chiles like habaneros, and wash hands well when you're done. Don't grind up seeds in a garbage disposal; the fumes are irritating to breathe. To roast fresh chiles: Roasting deepens flavor and lets the bitter skin slip off easier. Hold the chile with tongs over a gas flame or in the flame of a propane torch, or set on a very hot grill or under a broiler, until the skin fully blackens. Enclose in a plastic or paper bag, or put in a bowl and cover tightly with plastic wrap. Let cool about 15 minutes. Rub off the skin with your fingers or paper towels, then remove the stem and seeds. Alternatively, for a chile with more body for stuffing (but not as deep a flavor), drop the chile in hot oil (375°) until the skin blisters, 2 to 3 minutes. Remove from the oil, plunge into ice water, drain, and peel off the blistered skin. Use immediately or store in a plastic bag up to 2 days in the refrigerator or up to 1 month in the freezer.

Anaheim If a recipe calls for a "long green chile," this bright-green, tapered chile—and the very similar New Mexico green—is the one to use. Also called the California (it was first grown around Anaheim), it is 6 inches long and 2½ inches wide—a good choice for stuffing. It is widely available green, but less so ripe and red, which are more often dried and ground for chile powder.

Fresno Red While interchangeable with the red jalapeño, this is a separate variety and hotter. Also known as chile caribe, it is about 2 inches long and 1 inch at the shoulder.

Habanero While small—about 2 inches by 1½ inches—this is the hottest chile on earth. Ripe chiles are green and shades of orange to dark red. Handle it with TLC (and gloves), then harness its powerful heat and fruitiness in salsas, marinades, and as a pickled vegetable.

Hungarian Cherry Pepper This plump chile is about 1¾ inches round and a deep scarlet color. It is sweet and not too hot, good for salads and pickling.

Jalapeño This most popular green chile is a culinary workhorse—it improves any dish in need of some heat. Shiny green and tapered, it measures about 2 inches long and 1 inch wide. It's available canned as well as fresh. The red is sweeter and, when dried and smoked, is sold as a chipotle.

New Mexico A long green chile like the Anaheim, the medium-hot New Mexico measures 6 to 8 inches long and about 1½ inches across. But its flavor is hotter, sweeter, and deeper than the Anaheim, and further improved by roasting. The green chile is perfect for stuffing, and both the green and red forms are superb in sauces and salsas.

Poblano Blackish-green and pointy, this chile is 4 to 5 inches long and 2½ inches wide. Despite common mislabeling, it isn't a pasilla, which is a dried chilaca chile. It can be fiery. Always eaten roasted, it tastes earthy and smoky, and is big enough to stuff.

Serrano Ripe serranos are both green and red, 2 inches long and ½ inch wide. They heat up fresh salsas and cooked sauces.

Chile Relleno A Mexican dish, this is a large chile stuffed with cheese or other filling, dipped in batter, and deep-fried.

Chili A simmered concoction of meat, onions, chiles, spices, and often tomatoes, beans, and garlic. Also called chili con carne or "bowl of red."

Chili Powder and Chile Powder These are not the same, but many cooks think they are. "Chili" powder is a blend of sometimes dozens of types of ground dried red chiles with seasonings that include cumin, oregano, garlic, salt, and sometimes preservatives. It gives a bowl of chili its distinctive flavor. "Chile" powder is just that—dried red chile and nothing else. It is brick to dark red and varies in heat depending on the chile. Chile flakes, another form of seasoning, are crushed dried red chiles.

Chocolate The recipes in this book use chocolate in these forms. Store chocolate airtight in a cool, dry spot up to one year. Cocoa keeps indefinitely if well wrapped.

Bittersweet/Semisweet These chocolates are interchangeable, but bittersweet is more intensely chocolatey than semisweet and slightly less sweet. Use the best quality you can find. It makes a difference.

Dutch-Process Cocoa When cocoa is treated with an alkali to neutralize its acidity and mellow its flavor, it is "Dutched."

Mexican Chocolate This sweet grainy chocolate is flavored with ground almonds, cinnamon, and vanilla, and used most often in Mexico in a hot beverage.

Chorizo A spicy fresh pork sausage used in Mexican cooking that is seasoned many ways, but dried chiles, oregano, garlic, and cumin are common. Chorizo is sold in bulk or in links at Latino markets and well-stocked supermarkets. Remove the casing before cooking.

Cilantro The distinctive, almost musty pungency of cilantro (also sold as fresh coriander and Chinese parsley) marks many Mexican and Southwestern dishes. Use both the tender stems and leaves, but in salsas, the leaves alone look best. To trim: Rinse in a bunch under cold water; shake dry or drain on paper towels. When dry, hold by the stems and lay the bunch on its side on a cutting board. Slide a sharp chef's knife from stems to tips of leaves (mostly leaves will fall to the board) until you have what you need. Chop up the leaves and use. Refrigerate the leftover bunch, wrapped in paper towels and plastic wrap.

Citrus Abundant in the Southwest, lemons, limes, and oranges give food a fresh, lively taste. To zest: Remove the colored zest—the flavorful, outermost layer of the skin—with the coarse teeth of a grater (cover the teeth with parchment or waxed paper). Rub the fruit across the teeth, then pull off the zest-covered paper. Or lightly pull across the skin with a zester, a handheld peeler that pulls off threads of zest to then chop up with a knife. To juice: To get the most juice, first roll the fruit on a counter a few times, or microwave for a few seconds. Ream lemons and limes with a wooden citrus juicer, or squeeze by hand, catching the seeds with your fingers. Juicing large oranges and grapefruit is easiest with an electric juicer.

Comal The traditional griddle for cooking tortillas, sold in Latino markets. Substitute a cast-iron or heavy nonstick skillet.

Corn In Southwestern cooking, corn is a key ingredient. It's eaten fresh on and off the cob, and dried as hominy, masa harina, and cornmeal. Along with squash and beans, corn is one of the holy trinity of Native American ingredients. Buy the freshest corn you can find for best flavor. To remove fresh kernels from the cob: Stand the ear on its stem end. Cut down from the top with a sharp knife to slice off the kernels. Repeat all around the cob. To "milk" the cob for chowders, stews, and casseroles, scrape the bare cob again, catching the liquid in a bowl. To grill in the husk: Pull down the husk, but leave it attached to the cob. Remove the silks, then soak the ears in water 15 minutes or more (so they don't burn on the grill). Drain, pull the husk up, and grill over high heat until the corn is cooked, about 15 minutes. Remove husk and serve.

Corn Husks These dried, papery corn jackets, which keep steamed foods moist, are the wrappers for tamales, or fillings of meat, poultry, seafood, or vegetables, and must be softened to use. To soften: Soak in warm water 1 to 2 hours; drain on paper towels. To make a corn husk "boat" (an easy, attractive container for food): Tear strips from a softened corn husk. For each boat, tie off one end of a softened husk with a strip. If made up to a day ahead, stack the boats and wrap with plastic wrap to keep them moist.

Cornmeal Ground from dried yellow, white, or blue corn kernels, cornmeal is a versatile ingredient used in the Southwest for breads, pancakes, stews, and as a coating for fried foods. Blue cornmeal is a uniquely Southwestern product.

Cumin The golden, aromatic seed of a plant in the parsley family, cumin's aroma and flavor are distinctive and spicy. It is a basic seasoning in chili powders. For maximum punch, buy cumin seeds, not powder, and grind them at home (see **Grinding Spices**).

Enchilada A baked Mexican casserole of soft corn tortillas filled with cheese, meat, chicken, or fish and topped with a sauce.

Epazote In bean dishes, this pungent New World herb helps reduce gastric distress and can be an acquired taste. Also called stinkweed and wormweed, it grows wild in Mexico and the Southwest. Latino groceries often carry the dried herb, if not the fresh.

Fajitas Strips of marinated steak, chicken, or seafood quickly cooked on a very hot skillet or grill, and served with flour tortillas, grilled onions, peppers, guacamole, and salsa.

Flauta A corn tortilla rolled around a meat or chicken filling, then deep-fried and usually served with guacamole, salsa, and sour cream.

Garlic Both roasted and raw garlic are favorite Southwestern ingredients. To roast a head of garlic: Cut off the very top of the stem end of the head. Rub the cut end of the head with about 1 teaspoon of olive oil, wrap in aluminum foil, and bake at 350° until soft, 45 minutes to 1 hour. Remove from the foil and squeeze out the softened garlic to use as a spread or in a recipe. To peel cloves: The flat side of a chef's knife or the bottom of a heavy pan works best. Put unpeeled cloves on a work surface, then whack them with the knife or pan. The cloves will slide out easily from their skins. To crush: Hit the peeled cloves again with the knife or pan. To mince: Cut the cloves into strips, first horizontally, then vertically. Line up strips and cut across into small dice. Chop as finely as desired.

Grinding Spices Freshly ground whole spices are the most flavorful. To machine grind: Grind them in a coffee grinder reserved for spices, a spice grinder, or a mini food processor. To remove the taste of the spice from the grinder, fill with raw white rice and grind again. To hand-grind: Crush in a mortar with a pestle.

Guacamole A Mexican and Southwestern relish or dip made with mashed avocado, chiles, tomatoes, lime or lemon juice, onions, and sometimes cilantro and garlic. Alongside, you will find chips, tacos, quesadillas, raw vegetables, flautas, fajitas, and more.

Hominy To make hominy, corn kernels are soaked in slaked lime or lye to remove their germs and hulls, then dried. In the corn cultures of the Southwest—both Native American and Mexican—hominy appears in many traditional dishes, including the stew posole (hominy itself is also called "posole" in the Southwest). Hominy is sold dried (soak in water overnight to reconstitute), canned, and in plastic bags at Latino markets. Native Seeds/SEARCH (see Mail-Order Sources, page 217) sells exotic blue and red posole. When coarsely ground, dried hominy becomes grits.

Huevos Rancheros Poached or fried eggs on corn or flour tortillas, topped with a red or green sauce.

Jalapeño Jelly A popular condiment sold in Southwestern supermarkets with a vibrant color (green, red, or both) and sweet-hot flavor. A recipe is on page 33.

Jicama Dubbed the Mexican potato, this root vegetable is slightly sweet and nutty. Beneath the thick brown skin (always peeled away) is a creamy flesh with a refreshing crunch and texture perfect for salads or crudités. When cooked, it holds its crispness. Plentiful all year, it keeps well if refrigerated.

Julienne Food cut like matchsticks for eye appeal and uniform cooking are called julienne. Raw carrots, potatoes, squash, and jicama are often cut this way. To julienne: Use a very sharp knife. Cut food into ⅛-inch-thick slices. Stack the slices and cut them lengthwise into ⅛-inch strips, then cut the strips crosswise to the desired length.

Mango An ovoid tropical fruit with a large, flat seed and sweet, golden flesh. A ripe mango has reddish-yellow skin, very aromatic golden flesh, and is slightly soft to the touch (but some varieties are ripe even when hard). To peel: Stand the fruit on its broader end, narrow side facing you. Slice top to bottom about ½ inch on either side of the stem (to clear the seed; discard seed). To cube: Score the flesh into squares, but don't cut through the skin. Invert the skin to pop up the cubes, then slice them free with a paring knife.

Masa The Spanish word for dough, but specifically the corn dough used to make tortillas and tamales. To make masa, corn kernels are heated and soaked in a lime solution, washed, and ground. Latino markets and tortilla factories sell fresh masa.

Masa Harina A flour made from grinding dried corn dough (masa). Add water and salt, and use in any recipe that calls for masa. Most supermarkets stock it near wheat flour.

Mole A complex Mexican sauce usually for chicken, made with onion, garlic, chiles, ground seeds, and sometimes chocolate.

Nacho An appetizer of tortilla chips topped always with cheese, and sometimes chiles, beans, or meat, that is broiled until bubbly and hot.

Nopales/Nopalitos These pale to dark green, fleshy, thorny pads of the prickly pear cactus taste like tart green beans. They're delicious in salads, chiles, and casseroles. Fresh nopales are common in Southwestern groceries. Nopalitos—diced or sliced nopales—are sold canned in water or pickled in jars in larger supermarkets and Latino groceries. To prepare fresh pads: Remove needles and "eyes" with a vegetable peeler. With a sharp knife, cut ⅛ inch off the outer edge of each pad and discard. Cut the cleaned pad into thin strips (nopalitos) and use. To blanch: Drop strips in boiling water 1 to 2 minutes; plunge in ice water to stop cooking, then drain and use in a recipe.

Papaya A pear-shaped tropical fruit native to North America with a golden skin and juicy orange flesh. Its center cavity is packed with black seeds that are edible, but usually discarded. To prepare: Peel with a vegetable peeler, halve, and scoop out the seeds. Slice or cube the flesh.

Pecans A native American nut, related to the hickory, that grows throughout the South and the Southwest, particularly in Texas. The kernel is high in fat, with a buttery taste enhanced by toasting (see **Toasting Nuts and Seeds**). Pecans add crunch to salsas, salads, breads, and desserts.

Pepitas Dark green, hulled pumpkin seeds, pepitas are a favorite Southwestern ingredient and snack. Enjoy toasted and salted, or raw and ground in moles, sauces, and pestos. Buy pepitas at Latino markets.

Piñon Nuts The cones of the piñon pine, the state tree of New Mexico, yield these creamy, delicate nuts. They suit every course, soup to dessert. The Zuni and other tribes grind them into a fine meal to make bread. Whole piñons taste best toasted (see **Toasting Nuts and Seeds**). Refrigerate or freeze them so they won't get rancid. Use Italian pine nuts if you can't find piñon nuts.

Posole A thick soup made with pork or sometimes chicken, chiles, onions, garlic, and hominy (called "posole" in the Southwest). It's a feast-day dish for Native Americans, and appears on many Southwestern tables at Christmas and New Year. The recipe is on page 72.

Prickly Pear Fruit Also called a tuna, this purple, egg-shaped fruit grows on the pads of the prickly pear cactus. The rich magenta flesh is sweet and studded with edible (but very hard) black seeds, with a melonlike perfume. It's usually puréed and strained to remove the seeds, then used in sauces or drinks, as a syrup, or a coloring agent. To prepare: Peel the fruit with a sharp knife and purée the flesh in a food processor, then strain out the seeds. Prickly pear fruit is sold most of the year in the Southwest, and in Latino markets occasionally in other areas. Buy them slightly soft, with a uniform, dark red color.

Quesadilla The grilled cheese sandwich of Mexico and the Southwest uses tortillas for bread. To make: Sprinkle half of a tortilla with cheese, chiles, and any other filling, such as chicken or vegetables, then fold it over and grill. Serve in wedges with salsa, sour cream, or guacamole.

Salsa, Salsa Fresca An uncooked relish made of chopped vegetables or fruit, chiles, and spices to scoop up with a tortilla chip or to garnish various dishes. The best versions mix colors, textures, and flavors. Traditional salsa includes chopped tomatoes, onions, chiles, cilantro, lime juice, and sometimes garlic.

Squash Blossoms Sacred symbol to the Pueblos, the flowers of the squash plant are delicate and extremely fragile.

They should be picked before they open in the morning and used by the end of the day. To extend their freshness by a day, wrap them carefully in damp paper towels and refrigerate. The blossoms are stuffed with cheese or other filling, dipped in batter, and sautéed or deep-fried. Strips are scattered as a garnish, or used as a filling for quesadillas. Find them from April to September in specialty groceries.

Squeeze Bottle Almost every chef, Southwestern included, loves this grocery store gadget (aka a plastic ketchup or mustard bottle). They fill it with a purée or sauce, and squeeze out stunning patterns on the plate. Any home cook can do the same with a little practice.

Taco A crispy, open Mexican tortilla sandwich shaped like a U, filled with meat, chicken, fish, beans, and more, and usually topped with shredded lettuce, cheese, tomatoes, and salsa.

Tamale For this traditional Mexican dish, a filling is surrounded by masa (corn dough), wrapped in a corn husk, and steamed. The husks are removed before eating. Countless dozens are made at Christmas to eat and to give as gifts.

Tequila A potent, colorless spirit named for Tequila, a colonial town near Guadalajara, and distilled from the agave plant. The Spanish refined the process, but the Aztecs already knew how to prepare a mildly fermented drink from agave juice. Essential in the Southwest and elsewhere for margaritas and shots, now tequila even sparks marinades, desserts, and sauces. Tequila quality varies—the best is made from only blue agave (agave azul).

Toasting Nuts and Seeds To toast in a skillet: For seeds such as coriander, cumin, pepitas, or peppercorns, cook in a dry, hot skillet until aromatic and slightly brown (they sometimes pop), 3 to 5 minutes. To toast in the oven: For nuts, scatter on a baking sheet and bake at 350°, until fragrant and slightly brown, 5 to 10 minutes.

Tomatillo The Mexicans call them tomate verde (green tomatoes), and they look like green cherry tomatoes in a papery brown husk. But they're related to ground cherries, with a tart flavor and firm texture. Tomatillos are widely used in Mexico and the Southwest—fresh in salsas, and cooked in sauces, soups, and main dishes. Some groceries carry fresh tomatillos, but most sell them canned. To use: Remove the husk, then rinse the fruit well. To roast: For deeper flavor, roast the husked, rinsed fruit on a hot grill or over an open flame until slightly charred.

Tomato Another New World food, tomatoes appear in many Southwestern dishes. Some chefs peel them, but most only remove the seeds, then cut them into dice. To peel: Cut an X at the bottom of the tomato and drop in boiling water, 1 to 2 minutes. Plunge in ice water, then slip off the skin when cool. To core: Cut around the stem with a paring knife pointed toward the tomato's center until the core is released as a plug; discard. To seed: Halve across the middle. Hold one half over the sink and squeeze; the seeds will pop out. To roast: Hold the tomato (don't peel) over an open flame or on a hot grill, or roast in a 450° oven, until the skin blackens slightly.

Tortilla Press This hinged, iron or cast-aluminum device with two flat disks is said to be a Spanish invention to "automate" making tortillas, a laborious process when done by hand. To use, first line both disks with plastic wrap to make them nonstick. Place a ball of dough on the bottom disk, lower the top, then squeeze gently to flatten.

Vanilla Bean The pod of an orchid plant, vanilla grows only in tropical regions, including parts of Mexico (the Aztecs grew it). It must be hand-cultivated, so it's costly. The inside of the pod is soft, with tiny black seeds. Both pod and seeds are flavoring agents. To use: Cut the pod in half. Scrape out the seeds (usually into a pan of sauce or custard), then also drop in the pod (discard a cut pod after cooking; a whole pod can be reused). Vanilla beans are sold in jars or tubes in the spice section. Use promptly, or store them airtight in the freezer or refrigerator.

Mail-Order Sources

Bueno Foods
2001 Fourth Street
Albuquerque, NM 87102
(800) 95-CHILE (800-952-4453) (toll free)
Fax: (505) 242-1680
www.buenofoods.com
>*Blue cornmeal, fresh New Mexico green chiles (in season only), frozen chopped New Mexico green chiles, pure chile powders, red chile purée, ristras*

Chez Eynard, Ltd.
Phoenix, AZ
(602) 945-9528
Fax: (602) 945-9712
>*Chocolate, chorizo, fresh venison, mango purée, vanilla beans*

Melissa's Specialty Foods
World Variety Produce, Inc.
P.O. Box 21127
Los Angeles, CA 90021
(800) 588-0151 (toll free)
www.melissas.com
>*Achiote (annatto) seeds, corn husks, cumin seeds, dried chiles, dried beans, epazote, pepitas (pumpkin seeds), pepper jelly, posole, salsas*

Mozzarella Company
2944 Elm Street
Dallas, TX 75226
(214) 741-4072
(800) 798-2954 (toll free)
Fax: (214) 741-4076
E-mail: mozzco@aol.com
>*Queso blanco and other Mexican and specialty cheeses*

Native Seeds/SEARCH
526 N. Fourth Avenue
Tucson, AZ 85705
(520) 622-5561
Fax: (520) 622-5591
E-mail: nxx@azstarnet.com
http://desert/net/seeds/catalog/home.htm
>*Blue cornmeal, dried beans, heirloom seeds, mesquite flour, posole*

Penzey's, Ltd.
P.O. Box 933
Muskego, WI 53150
(414) 679-7207
Fax: (414) 679-7878
>*Achiote (annato) seeds, cardamom seeds, chili powders, cumin seeds, dried chiles, epazote, ground chile powders, saffron, vanilla beans*

The Perfect Purée
Hayward Enterprises, Inc.
975 Vintage Avenue, Suite B
St. Helena, CA 94574
(800) 556-3707 (toll free)
Fax: (707) 967-8799
E-mail: purées@aol.com
www.perfectpurée.com
>*Prickly pear purée*

Seeds of Change
P.O. Box 15700
Santa Fe, NM 87506-5700
(888) 762-7333 (toll free)
>*Heirloom seeds*

Episode Descriptions

Tortillas in Everything

For centuries corn was the dominant grain of the Southwest. Flour was introduced when the Spanish brought wheat. Corn and flour tortillas, rather than bread, are staples of the Southwestern table, and there's nothing better than a home-made tortilla hot off the griddle. Barbara shows viewers how easy it is to prepare them. In the hands of French-trained Southwestern chef Vincent Guerithault, tortillas achieve haute cuisine status.

The Bounty of the Outdoors

Throughout the Southwest, lakes, rivers, and streams teem with fish; the forests yield wild turkey, deer, and elk; and the desert supports javelina, quail, and a bounty of wildlife. Hunting and fishing are popular pastimes in this scenic, diverse region. Barbara and chef Robert McGrath cook fresh trout riverside in Oak Creek Canyon—red rock country. Back in the kitchen, Barbara prepares a delicious fruit salsa and Robert demonstrates his Wild West cuisine.

Cactus

Chef Jay McCarthy is president of the Professional Association of Cactus Development and a world expert on cactus. He tells us all about the prickly pear cactus, the official state plant of Texas. The pads appear in salads, as a wrapper for stewed meats, even as French fries. The puréed fruit sweetens sorbets, margaritas, sauces, and salsas. Barbara demonstrates a delicious sorbet made with prickly pear fruit, and Jay cooks up some cactus, including his famous Cactus Rita, a magenta margarita.

Chocolate and Other Mexican Influences

The Aztec emperors used chocolate as an aphrodisiac. Today, modern Southwestern chefs include it, and other pre-Columbian ingredients, in a variety of dishes. Chocolate is the theme: Barbara pairs up chile and chocolate in a crunchy cookie. Chef and chocolate expert Donna Nordin prepares a modern-day chicken mole (chocolate is part of it), then elevates the lowly taco to an elegant chocolate dessert.

Local Produce

In recent years there has been a rebirth in the use of local produce in Southwestern cuisine. Thanks to talented chefs like Roxsand Scocos, who use unusual and just-picked produce in their restaurants, home cooks are now also searching for the freshest ingredients. Barbara grills sweet corn basted with a spicy butter, while Roxsand rolls up a harvest of fresh flavors in a crêpe.

Tamales

Tamales have been part of Southwestern cuisine for centuries. In pre-Hispanic times they were even sacred offerings to the deities. Tamales are a festive food, especially during the holidays when friends gather to make them by the tens of dozens. Using "nature's perfect wrapper," the corn husk, Barbara prepares a great main course for entertaining. John Rivera Sedlar, father of modern Southwestern cuisine, demonstrates tamales old and very new.

Dried Chiles

In New Mexico, cooks preserve ripe chiles to use throughout the winter by drying them on long strings called ristras. The dried chiles are picked from the garland, then ground into a powder to use as a seasoning, toasted, and plumped in water to toss in the soup pot, chopped up for salsas, or puréed for a sauce. From dried red New Mexico chiles, Barbara makes a Southwestern sauce with many uses. Chefs Mary Sue Milliken and Susan Feniger talk about the ancho and chipotle—their favorite dried chiles—then fire up a great menu.

Fresh Chiles

Fresh chiles are perhaps the most important component of Southwestern food. There is extensive lore surrounding the chile pepper. Its health benefits, for example, have long been promoted. A key to Southwestern cuisine is to know a small number of crucial techniques for preparing chiles. How to roast fresh chiles to enhance their flavor and slip off their skin is part of Barbara's recipe for Green Chile and Tomatillo Sauce. Texas chef Stephan Pyles updates chiles rellenos and gives bread pudding a devilish twist.

Green Chile and Tomatillo Sauce (page 195)
Goat Cheese and Crab Rellenos with Fiery Black Bean–Pineapple Salsa (page 108)
Chocolate Diablo Bread Pudding (page 176)

Beef, Southwestern Style

The Southwest has always been known for its cattle. In fact, several cows are even grazing a few blocks from Barbara's house in central Phoenix. But say "cattle," and it's usually Texas that comes to mind. Houston chef Robert Del Grande tells how to cook great beef with surefire success. But first Barbara demonstrates that other Texas specialty—chili con carne, prepared without beans the way the Lone Star State likes it.

Chili con Carne (page 74)
Coffee-Roasted Fillet of Beef with Pasilla Chile Broth (page 82)
Gratin of Swiss Chard (page 134)

The Three Sisters

The holy trinity of Native American cooking—corn, squash, and beans—is called the Three Sisters. These New World crops have sustained the peoples here for centuries. Chef Loretta Barrett Oden, a native Potawatomi, shares her culture and its cuisine. Barbara incorporates the delicate blossoms of the squash plant—revered by Native Americans—into a delicious filling for quesadillas.

Squash Blossom Quesadillas (page 24)
Three Sisters Stew with Corn Dumplings (page 66)
Indian Pudding (page 165)

Native Seeds and Heirloom Plants

The mass marketing of fruits and vegetables has resulted in the development of produce that is beautiful and resistant to disease, but often lacks flavor. Thanks to groups like Native Seeds/SEARCH and chefs like Janos Wilder, the long-forgotten delights of heirloom vegetables are again on Southwestern tables. Janos prepares two of his signature dishes that use heirlooms, while Barbara serves up the original Southwest comfort food—posole.

Traditional Posole (page 72)
Blue Corn–Crusted Cabrilla with Rainbow Posole Broth (page 112)
Salsa Fresca (page 198)

Outdoor Cooking

Cooking outdoors has always been part of the Southwestern lifestyle—today, for convenience, in the past, from necessity. For whatever reason, grilling over wood imparts an exceptional flavor to game, meat, fish, poultry, and vegetables. And when ovens aren't handy, try Dutch oven cooking for a rustic, outdoor meal. Chef Chuck Wiley—a modern-day cowboy—shows viewers how to be at home on the (outdoor) range. Barbara grills a rustic potato salad that gives a whole new dimension to the lowly spud.

Grilled Potato Salad (page 48)
Achiote-Basted Rack of Venison (page 86)
Roasted Vegetables (page 144)
Dutch Oven Green Chile Corn Bread (page 154)

Barbecue

Grilling is not barbecue. And barbecue is not grilling. One is cooking for a short time over a hot fire. The other—real barbecue—means long, slow cooking over indirect heat. Today's barbecue is not the mammoth affair it once was—involving whole animals smoked over fragrant wood coals for hours. Covered grills or brick smokers replace the traditional barbecue pit, and a spicy baste, not a wrap of wet burlap, keeps the meat moist and gives it some punch. Barbara makes guacamole, the ultimate Southwestern barbecue partner. Chef Lenard Rubin gives Spanish paella a Southwestern spin with plenty of barbecue (the noun, not the verb).

Guacamole (page 211)
Southwestern Barbecue Paella (page 103)

Index